Systems of Support in Education Settings

All classrooms have neurodivergent children and young people in them, and how you support them as a practitioner has a lasting impact. This book guides you in understanding and developing a system for supporting neurodiversity in your classroom.

The book introduces the concept of systems thinking to an education setting, providing tools and strategies to both broaden your knowledge of neurodiversity and to develop a framework to meet the needs of neurodivergent learners. Systems thinking will encourage you to get comfortable with uncertainty, to look for connections or patterns, and to be prepared to change if something isn't working. By increasing your awareness and remaining curious about the individual needs in your classroom, you will enrich the learning experience for all. Chapters guide you to make plans, change practices, and take risks for learners to progress – considering a constellation of skills – with carefully selected tasks and practical interventions to help you to know when to reflect, when to apply knowledge, and when to discuss further with colleagues.

Systems of Support in Education Settings introduces a system for you, with you and your learners at its heart. It provides a hands-on approach to supporting neurodiversity in primary and secondary classrooms and will be essential reading for teachers, both new and experienced, who are keen to improve and invest in effective practice.

Kelly Challis has spent her career in education advocating for neurodivergent people and currently leads a team of specialist assessors for a health care organisation. She has published articles in local press as well as for the PATOSS bulletin, a recognised body for specialist assessors. Her past roles included SENCo/Head of Learning Support, and education consultant supporting schools to develop high-quality literacy provision and raising awareness of neurodiversity. More recently, Kelly designed and implemented training programmes for middle leaders and teachers with a national charity to meet the needs of learners with literacy difficulties in primary and secondary education settings.

Systems of Support in Education Settings

Building Inclusive Learning Environments

Kelly Challis

LONDON AND NEW YORK

Designed cover image: Getty Images

First published 2026
by Routledge
4 Park Square, Milton Park, Abingdon, Oxon OX14 4RN

and by Routledge
605 Third Avenue, New York, NY 10158

Routledge is an imprint of the Taylor & Francis Group, an informa business

British Library Cataloguing-in-Publication Data
A catalogue record for this book is available from the British Library

ISBN: 978-1-032-50998-3 (hbk)
ISBN: 978-1-032-50996-9 (pbk)
ISBN: 978-1-003-40063-9 (ebk)

DOI: 10.4324/9781003400639

Typeset in Optima
by Apex CoVantage, LLC

Dedications

To my family, my husband Paul and two daughters, Eloise and Serena Summer. I love you all.

This book is dedicated to my brother Matthew who died in 2019. He had a rough time through school and left without many qualifications but later in life committed to becoming a police officer and worked his socks off to pass the exams. He studied and applied himself even though he found it hard and unfamiliar. It was one of the proudest moments of my life to see him achieve something he felt was off-limits to him.

I love you, Maff, and miss you every day.

Contents

Acknowledgements

To Gemma Archer, Laura Dobson, Bigi Luetchford, Dave Barrett, Sam Reynolds, Kate Paterson, Nikki Read, Lara Furmidge, Jenny Jones, Harriet Booth, Jo Robinson, thank you for giving up your time to add your perspective and share your expertise.

Introduction

A Letter from the Author

Dear practitioner,

Sometimes an experience alters our way of thinking, even while it is happening and sometimes it can be on reflection that we realise the impact it has had on our being and our outlook on life.

I was fortunate to enjoy my years in school, did well in exams and was the first person in my family to attend university, the second person being my eldest daughter, so higher education was not something I knew much about. As a free school meals child and later having my own experience of hardship as a young single mum, my learning journey has not been easy. As I meandered along a career path in education that took me through primary, secondary, alternative provision, further and higher education, I developed skills in supporting learners as well as teaching them.

During my time in leadership, one of the most significant challenges as a SENCo was to deliver the message to staff that some children need a different approach, with the backdrop of large classes, limited resourcing and numerous other demands on their time and energy.

Whilst working for a charity, I developed an online course for teachers and middle leaders to champion literacy. This course had systems thinking at its core and the cohorts I worked with were inspiring; their commitment to learning more about dyslexia and how to support learners in their settings was the ripple effect I set out to create.

The value of a systems thinking approach has continued to influence my ways of working and is the foundation of this book. It requires a curiosity and being prepared to explore and reflect little and often. A key facet of systems thinking is iterating – which has made finalising this book a challenge. A tweak here, addition there; the potential to titivate is endless. However,

DOI: 10.4324/9781003400639-1

systems thinking is fundamentally about action and I am content that there are learning opportunities, knowledge and reflections a-plenty within the pages of this book.

There are several case studies to show you how systems thinking can be applied to common situations in an educational setting:

Chapter 4 – Case Study 1: *A Dyslexic, Dyspraxic, ADHD Learner Struggling with Reading*

Chapter 5 – Case Study 2: *A 17-Year-Old Learner with Processing Difficulties Falling Behind in Science*

Chapter 6 – Case Study 3: *An NQT Planning a New Topic with Literacy Integration*

Chapter 7 – Case Study 4: *A Learner Who Finds It Difficult to Access Small Group Work*

Chapter 8 – Case Study 5: *A Family Applying for an EHCP*

Chapter 9 – Case Study 6: *A 14-Year-Old with Anxiety Struggling to Attend School*

As you work your way through the book you will be encouraged to apply systems thinking models, especially the viable systems model (VSM) which will be introduced in-depth in Chapter 1. This is your system of support and will provide a model which can be adapted, iterated on and applied to different cohorts and situations. It takes some time to understand but is worth the effort.

Each chapter informs at least one part of the system. You will be guided as to when there is an opportunity to add to the VSM during each chapter.

In addition to this, the Moments of Reflection are categorised as the following:

1. *Curiosity*
2. *Multiple perspectives*
3. *Interrelationships*
4. *Boundary Judgements*
5. *Practice*

These will maintain the focus on systems thinking and keep you questioning and evolving your practice as your progress through the book. There is also a checklist at the end of each chapter in case you have missed one.

Throughout the book are letters from practitioners who share their perspective on achieving a holistic approach to support in the classroom. Their words have not been changed by me and everyone was asked to share tips and strategies for education practitioners to support learners that find classroom tasks challenging. I am grateful for each and every one of these contributions and how they add to the constellation of perspectives and strategies for classroom practice.

Treat this book like a workbook; scribbling in the margins is positively encouraged.

It is recommended to buy a notebook dedicated to this book. Add reflections, drawings and plans but if writing isn't your thing, consider creating an electronic record of research, inspiring pictures and voice notes. This will not only help solidify the ideas in this book but also ensure that you reflect on the system of which you are a part and can, with often small actions, change.

Above all remain curious about this book; it does not promise definitive answers, but it does promise to nurture curiosity and support you in developing your practice for learners who struggle – at times, this struggle might include you and that is ok.

This approach has been influenced by the work of Dina Abbott (2007) in 'Doing "incorrect" research: The importance of the subjective and the personal in researching poverty'. Her reflection on the appropriateness of certain research practices given the context has shaped how this book does not shy away from subjectivity and knowing the value of your own personal experience but also its limitations. In Chapter 2, there is the opportunity to reflect on your own values but also your potential biases and to start to confront these. To foster a person-centred approach does not mean you will wholly understand their point of view or that you need to know their entire life history to empathise. By being open, curious and listening without judgement you will meet them where they are rather than where you perceive they should be.

Privilege and Perspective

In systems thinking, it is often unexpected feedback that reveals hidden structures. Abbott's (2007) narrative offers such a moment, capturing how a simple question exposed the deep structures of poverty and privilege.

Abbott (2007, p. 226) tells a story about how her privilege was starkly highlighted when a woman in her research asked her how many children she had, and followed this up with a further question – how many had died.

The matter of fact tone of this question (which recurred several times), and my own startled response to something I would never have dreamt of asking anyone at home, told me more about poverty (and my privilege) than any amount of quantitative data on the subject of infant mortality.

Like Abbott, I came to understand the reality of systemic inequality not through statistics, but through a moment of lived experience that cut through assumptions and data. I was tutoring a boy on a bricklaying course. He had recently been made homeless and was living in a hostel. He was often late to class and he therefore would have to forfeit his Education Maintenance Allowance due to poor attendance. This would mean he couldn't afford to get to college; a vicious cycle and one which would inevitably result in him dropping out of the course. He was severely dyslexic but engaging, verbose and intelligent. His commitment to the course meant that he would walk over six miles to a train station and dodge the conductor in order to get to college. This could be seen as tenacity and grit but in reality, it was a survival strategy and one which was unlikely to be sustainable. Understanding the complexity of a situation can put the spotlight on feedback loops which, if broken, could change a person's learning experience.

Throughout the book are figures which include hand-drawn images. I could have chosen to include digital images only but systems thinking is not about perfection but iteration and exploration so first drafts of ideas have been included alongside diagrams and tables.

Engage with the material, hold it lightly and stay curious.
Kelly

Reference

(1) Abbott, D. (2007). Doing 'incorrect' research: the importance of the subjective and the personal in researching poverty. In A. Thomas & G. Mohan (Eds), *Research skills for policy and development: How to find out fast* (pp. 208–226). Sage.

1

Building a System of Support

Overview

This chapter lays the groundwork for a **systems thinking** approach in education – an approach that sees learners, classrooms, policies and practitioners as part of an interconnected whole. Rather than prescribing one-size-fits-all interventions, it invites you to slow down, look closer and consider the interrelationships, multiple perspectives and boundary judgements that shape education experiences.

This chapter introduces practical tools and models to help you make sense of complexity, navigate uncertainty, and design flexible, inclusive responses to learner needs.

Systems thinking; an approach to support change in education settings

This chapter introduces systems thinking in-depth with the intention that you will then be able to use this approach throughout the rest of the book. It uses the English education system as its context and refers to the following regulations:

- **The Education Act (2011)**
- **SEND Code of Practice (2014)**

It will use the term 'learner/s', and recommendations are for all children and young people, and it will use the term 'practitioner/s' to avoid limiting the approach to teachers. It will attempt not to exclude anyone interested in developing systems for learning on the basis of job title or experience.

DOI: 10.4324/9781003400639-2

Provided within this chapter are a few ways of working from systems thinking which can support a deeper understanding of your practice. There are many models in the discipline but those selected for this book are cumulative and form part of an approach which is explained in detail later in the chapter. Please bear in mind that what is shared here is the tip of the iceberg when it comes to systems thinking. What is encouraged is a sense of curiosity and playfulness to experiment with the models and reflect on what might work for you and your practice.

Fostering a 'Do Now' Approach to Support

Systems thinking offers a bridge between identifying the areas of difficulty a learner may have and any formal intervention. It is intended to support action which is considered and informed by the practitioner and fundamentally facilitate a greater understanding of that learner, irrespective of labels or potential future diagnoses.

Equally this approach is intended to support everyone in the classroom as it recognises that learning and the associated skills are not developed in a linear fashion and can be affected by social, emotional, environmental and behavioural factors. Whilst some of these differences can be predicted and mitigated for, such as undiagnosed special educational needs and disabilities (SEND) or looked-after children, many are unforeseen and impossible to plan for and therefore need an approach which can absorb such dips without it impacting their overall performance.

Moment of Reflection 1.1: Interrelationships

Reflect on a cohort or your class and consider their learning and whether any of them follow a clear linear trajectory when developing their skills. For example, they learn to spell a word by recognising the phonics patterns or letter patterns and can accurately write this word without much thought. The progression in this skill is then writing it in a sentence. This would be the expected development of someone's ability to spell. A spiky trajectory may have the learner take longer to write the word successfully, experience inconsistencies when practising the word and find it difficult to write in a sentence without having to think about it carefully or ask for help. It is likely you will have learners with a variety of skills and abilities and these will not be fixed or subject dependent. This exercise is intended to build awareness of these differences, not to address them all. What is the scope of need in your classroom? Are there subjects or topics which require more support than others?

Key Points to Keep in Mind Throughout the Book

1. Repeated themes of systems thinking: Interrelationships, multiple perspectives, and boundary judgements.
2. Appreciating the complexity of learning for all its moving parts and identifying solutions which embrace this complexity and work with it.
3. Maintaining an approach that is agile and flexible to meet the needs of all in the classroom.

Figure 1.1 The foundations of systems thinking

The Cycle of a Teacher

For as long as I can remember, my year has started in September and terms often replaced seasons. The summer holidays would be a combination of relaxing and de-stressing after a busy year and planning/looking ahead to the next year. Lessons would need planning for at least the first six weeks of term for existing students and assimilating the profiles of the newcomers to the school. As the end of term arrived in July there would always be one eye trained on September and if I am honest, an apprehension about the level of busyness that would accompany the new term.

It can often be easy to forget those plans for being organised and less reactive as the demands of the classroom take over and the joy of the first couple of inset days to prepare are soon a distant memory when the corridors are full of children and school staff.

Building a Practice of Reflection

Taking some time, even ten minutes a couple of times a week, to reflect on what is really happening in your setting will be time well spent.

Figure 1.2 An image of a person thinking about themselves thinking

Systems thinking takes reflection one step further and encourages reflection not only on the events and major players but also your role in the process. Almost like your own bird's eye view. Becoming a **reflexive practitioner** requires humble reflection on your own involvement.

Moment of Reflection 1.2: Practice

Consider setting some time aside at the beginning of your day to reflect on the day ahead. Write as freely as you can (if you prefer, make voice notes) recording your intentions for the day, your mood/ feelings and your plan.

Later, reflect on those early notes and how the day unfolded. You might want to add in some gratitude there but you're looking for patterns, when you have completed several reflections, are there themes emerging which can help you better predict how a day might unfold? Can you pinpoint if it's your practice or the group dynamics? etc.

Systems Thinking and Its Practical Application

Systems thinking is a way of understanding the world that sees everything as interconnected. Small changes in one part of a system can have big consequences for the whole system, but we might not see the impact of those changes for a while, if at all.

Whilst the foundations of systems thinking are **interrelationships**, **boundary judgements** and **multiple perspectives** which lend themselves to application in many situations, systems thinking's roots are in cybernetics which led to the development of models that intend to explain the communication both inside and outside of a system.

We will be exploring a few models during the course of this book; their application can be wide ranging and they can be used again and again.

Systems thinking promises to maintain a fluid approach to situations and eschews the conventions of target setting. It requires agility from the actors involved and humility, particularly from those in positions of power, as they are often confronted with the origins of that power and are encouraged to question long-held beliefs.

Moment of Reflection 1.3: Interrelationships

How is feedback gathered at your setting? Does this include feedback up the hierarchy as well as down? What impact does this feedback have on practice?

To illustrate the impact of systems thinking, below is an example of how it has been used to address climate change. Whilst this example is not education based it outlines how systems thinking tackles such a big, worldwide problem. To illustrate the application of systems thinking the example of the UN's Sustainable Development Goals has been used.

There are 17 goals, and goal 13 is for climate action (UN, n.d.). There are five targets in goal 13, which are shown in Table 1.1.

Table 1.1 The Sustainable Development Goals and how to approach them

Sustainable Development Goal 13 targets	*Systems thinking approach*
13.1 Strengthen resilience and adaptive capacity to climate-related hazards and natural disasters in all countries	Building resilience by getting comfortable with uncertainty
13.2 Integrate climate change measured in national policies	Build consensus and collaboration
13.3 Improve education	Design more effective solutions
13.a Address the needs of developing countries through meaningful mitigation actions and operationalise the Green Climate Fund	Consensus and collaboration
13.b Promote mechanisms for raising capacity in the least developed countries and small island developing states with an emphasis on women, youth and local and marginalised communities.	Identifying leverage points for change

Climate change is such a huge, messy, interrelated and complex issue that it is attractive to systems thinking. Below is a suggestion on how it might be used to explore such a topic:

- **Identify leverage points for change:** Leverage points are places in a system where a small change can have a big impact. Systems thinking can help us to identify these leverage points and to focus our efforts on them.
- **Design more effective solutions:** Systems thinking can help us to design solutions that take into account the full complexity of the climate change problem. This can help us to avoid unintended consequences and to achieve our goals more effectively.
- **Build consensus and collaboration:** Systems thinking can help us to build consensus and collaboration around climate change solutions. By understanding the different perspectives and interests involved, we can develop solutions that are more likely to be adopted and implemented.

In addition to the above, here are some other ways that systems thinking can be used to address climate change:

- **Educating the public about climate change:** Systems thinking can be used to develop educational materials that help people to understand the complexity of climate change and the importance of taking action.
- **Informing decision making:** Systems thinking can be used to inform decision making at all levels, from individual choices to government policies.
- **Managing risks:** Systems thinking can be used to identify and manage risks associated with climate change, such as the risk of extreme weather events or the risk of sea level rise.
- **Building resilience:** Systems thinking can be used to build resilience to the impacts of climate change, such as by developing more sustainable infrastructure or by adapting agricultural practices.

As you can see, there are several opportunities with the development goals and a systems thinking approach to find solutions for complex, global issues.

Moment of Reflection 1.4: Practice

Before reading on, consider how these strategies could be applied to education.

Scribble down some ideas around these headings:

- Identifying leverage points
- Designing more effective solutions
- Building consensus and collaboration
- Informing decision making
- Managing risks
- Building resilience

Consider how these strategies could be applied to education:

- Embrace the changing nature of education and all its complexities. Avoiding narrow and restrictive directives enables an easier transition from one strategy to another.
- Gives a high level of reflection for professional development. This can be the whole school and valuable continuing professional development (CPD). The more cross-curricular, the better.
- Move away from fixed targets which some individuals do not fit.
- Identify leverage points in education which are small changes that can make a big impact. This is the purpose of this book as it is education practitioners who can identify and address these leverage points and be the first to act.
- Managing risk. If schools gain a broader understanding of how the systems of their school work together, they will be able to manage risk more efficiently.
- Educating: The school–home dynamic is often difficult to maintain and to get right. An approach that leaves assumptions at the door and fosters an openness to different perspectives will build trust and deepen the foundations of this relationship making more difficult conversation easier.
- Build consensus: Enabling more conversations through and across departments will allow more voices to be heard and ideas to be shared. This approach encourages openness and is likely to result in more collaboration and agreement to accept change.

Embracing the Messy

Systems thinking recognises that the world we live in is messy and complex. It avoids looking for solutions to problems, and instead analyses situations; the whole approach is iterative, and rather than mitigating uncertainty it makes it part of the process. Its purpose is not *'to do what you've always done'* but *'know what you do when you do what you do'*. There is a subtle difference which will become clearer as you progress through the chapters.

The reframing of problems as situations in itself has appeal as not only does it reduce the search for a single solution but it also shares the load and makes everyone involved a player rather than the source of a problem, which can lead to a blame culture.

Thinking about a situation rather than a problem immediately prompts consideration of the actors involved, context and factors at play rather than reducing what is happening to a collection of words which end in a question mark.

This can be seen throughout education, for example in attendance. Any parent of a child with mental health challenges or SEND will tell you that they would love their child to have regular attendance, but at times that is impossible. More often than not, the reason for poor attendance is not the parent's lack of interest in getting their children to school every day. If the

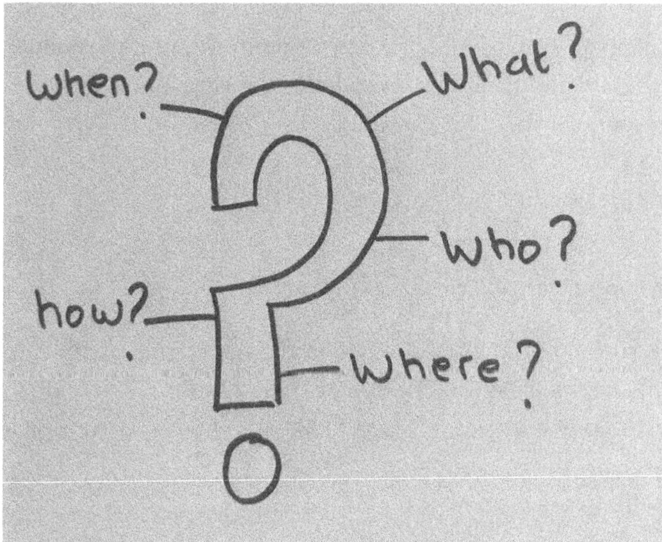

Figure 1.3 The 5 'w' questions

focus is on attendance due to a lack of attainment, a learning need might be being overlooked or there could be a home situation which is making attendance challenging. Adding more pressure to attend may result in a complete breakdown in the relationship between learner and school. When I was at school, I had to take the service bus and I had a choice: either arrive at school too early and hang around in all weathers till the doors opened, or sometimes arrive a little late to register. As I grew older, the latter option became the preferred one and I took the consequences of late marks on the chin. My lateness was in no way related to my attainment. It was a difficult choice but one which did not need to result in punishment if my tutor had enquired about my lateness and the reason for it.

Moment of Reflection 1.5: Curiosity

Think of a time when a behaviour – yours or someone else's – was misunderstood because the full context wasn't known. What might have changed if someone had asked curious, compassionate questions instead of making an assumption?

Exploring the Foundations of Systems Thinking in Greater Depth

Systems thinking enables those in education to respond to situations with increased agility and flexibility. In order to develop a deeper understanding of the three key facets of systems thinking – interrelationships, multiple perspectives and boundary judgements – these will be explored through the following situation.

Understanding Interrelationships

Situation: Your school has decided to implement a trial of all learners to line up outside the classroom before all their lessons.

The first step in applying systems thinking in your classroom will be to consider how things work together or potentially in conflict with one another with an open mind.

The advantages to the lining up before lessons strategy:

- Popular and widely used strategy: It is common practice in many education settings.
- A sense of calm before lessons: The learners will be better prepared for learning and to enter quietly into a calm frame of mind after a break or lunch, possibly spent running around, full of energy.
- Established routine: This routine will signal to the learner that the classroom environment is different to the playground or home and is a place of study and study needs quiet and stillness.
- Collective aim: It reinforces the collective responsibility for a classroom atmosphere conducive to working as entrance to the classroom is unlikely to happen until ALL learners are quiet and waiting in an orderly fashion.

Sounds like a good plan, but to implement such a strategy, some groundwork needs to be completed, as there will be several learners who, without any preparation, will take longer to accept this new approach.

Understanding cause and effect invites reflection on **what the behaviour policy is trying to achieve** – and whether the approach chosen aligns with values such as inclusion, equity and psychological safety.

Moment of Reflection 1.6: Curiosity

Consider the following learners and reflect upon their experience of this strategy. Does it change your perspective of the strategy?

The Learner Who Has Lots of Energy

They've spent the last 20–30 minutes running around and are hot and sweaty. That residual energy is still in their bodies, and they are struggling to slow down. This will be both a physiological and neurological feeling which may take longer than lining up time to regulate.

The Learner Who Finds It Hard to Regulate Their Emotions

There was an incident at break time and a falling out amongst friends. This learner will be ruminating over the event and may find it hard to put those intrusive thoughts to one side in order to settle to learning without speaking to a trusted adult first.

The Learner Who Finds It Hard to Remember Routines

They rely on their friends for behavioural cues and those friends are in another part of the line. This causes some anxiety, and they find it hard to remember what they are meant to do until they have practised it several times. They may queue jump in order to find those trusted buddies which will cause disruption.

The Learner Who Finds It Hard to Stand Up Without Swaying Due to Proprioceptive Difficulties

Some learners find it difficult to ground themselves and need stimulation from swaying to understand their space in the world. Standing and sitting still can therefore be challenging without the support of feedback from a wall, a chair or the ground. This may result in leaning, touching the physical space around them or swinging their arms, all of which can be interpreted as disruption.

Before implementing any decision which will impact everyone, consider how it will look and feel for different members of the classroom. The intent may be thoughtful and for the right reasons, but the implementation may need careful planning and rehearsal in order to be successful.

Engaging with Multiple Perspectives

Before you can consider multiple perspectives you need to establish what **stakeholders** you are working with. Why not also consider the influence and impact those stakeholders may have on your teaching practice?

This can be achieved by completing a stakeholder matrix and this will help you consider who needs to know what and when. A stakeholder matrix, if you are unfamiliar, is a strategic tool to understand the level of interest and influence key actors in a situation have.

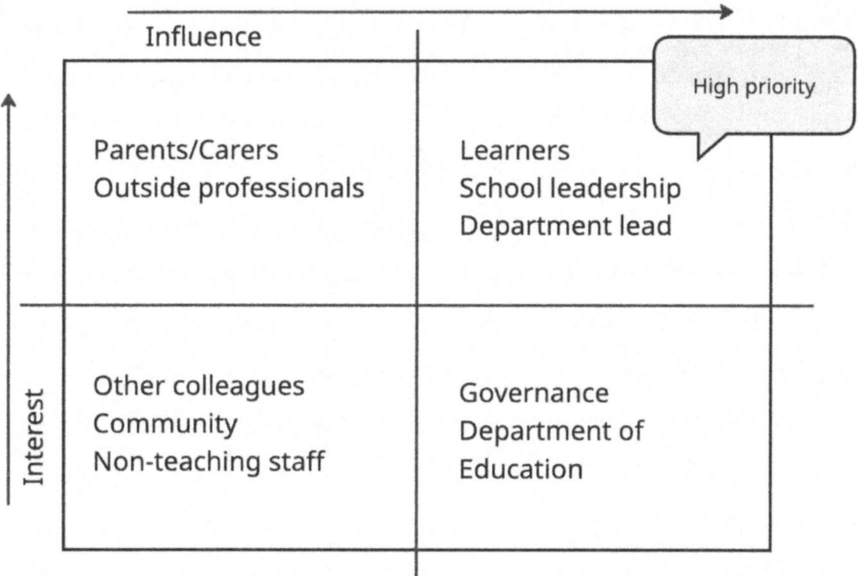

Figure 1.4 A stakeholder matrix

High Influence / High Interest: These stakeholders require active management and close engagement.
High Influence / Low Interest: These stakeholders need keeping in the loop and information can be selected for relevance.
Low Influence / High Interest: Provide updates and accept feedback.
Low Influence / Low Interest: They require minimal engagement but should not be ignored as their status might change.

Moment of Reflection 1.7: Multiple Perspectives

Consider the ways you communicate with the groups in Figure 1.4. Is it the same method? Could your chosen method be changed to suit the group more closely? For example, a briefing document for the high influence group or a weekly newsletter for the high influence / high interest group; and for the low interest / low influence group, updates on the setting's website?

Once you have decided who your stakeholders are, the next step is to consider their perspectives in your classroom. You might find as a newly qualified teacher, there's a lot of guidance and it's challenging to deviate from what is being advised, especially when you are being assessed or graded. Conversely as a senior leader, you may want more feedback or guidance at times, but your peers are reluctant to provide it in case of perceived repercussions. There might be certain times of the year when feedback is gathered from certain stakeholders, and what impact will this have on their feedback?

You might consider some elements of your practice out of bounds for comment and perhaps that is quite right too, but interrogate the why behind that decision.

If you are considering stakeholders in your school community, think about everyone who considers the buildings their place of work. This might also include those who use it outside school hours and during school holidays. The wider you cast the net to collect perspectives, the broader the understanding. You never know who you might learn from. It is difficult to separate multiple perspectives from interrelationships, and a significant disconnect between these two elements will impact on the overall success of the system itself.

Reframing Relationships

The parent/carer and practitioner relationship can be pivotal in supporting a learner's progress. What needs to be agreed is a collective understanding of a child's needs which can sometimes be difficult to achieve. Parents/carers want the best for their child and they can be apprehensive about the future if they have been told that their child is struggling or may have some learning difficulties. Such news can derail the plans which parents/carers might have had mapped out in their head for their child.

It is often the role of learning support to mediate between the parents and the other school staff as well as manage the parents' expectations. They can also be the team to initially identify the learner's specific learning needs and address them through targeted support.

Some ideas on how to manage parent/carer relationships:

1. Coffee mornings: Invite the parents/carers in and address their concerns as a group. Often they hear similar stories from other parent/carers and learn most from them.

2. Information sessions: How does your subject work? What is phonics? How do you use the 'bus stop method' for example.
3. Meetings with children and parents with the emphasis on collaboration rather than informing.
4. Cross-curricular discussions: Learn more about a learner's behaviour in other subjects and analyse the similarities and differences to their experience in your classroom.
5. Monthly newsletters: Keep the parents informed and engaged with you and build a community.

Reflecting on Boundary Judgements

Let's consider boundary judgements in relation to the classroom and how these may impact on a practitioner's decision making regarding support for those with literacy difficulties.

There can be a hesitance to implement any changes when a learner's needs have been identified by a class teacher and a referral to the SENCo has been made in case any intervention made is the wrong one or their difficulties worsen as a result of a new strategy.

If you have identified a need in the classroom YOU are the best-placed person to address this, and whilst further assessment of that learner's needs will clarify what support they need, being mindful and reflective about what is preventing their progress in the classroom will ONLY be helpful.

To address this boundary, consider the following:

1. What is the time frame on the learner being assessed? If it is a couple of weeks, then monitor their progress for any signs of dips in self-confidence or reluctance to participate and wait for recommendations.
2. If it is likely to be more than a couple of weeks, consider doing the following:
    - Speak with the learner and get their perspective on what they are struggling with.
    - Complete a classroom audit of the surroundings, the curriculum and your delivery of information. Is there anything which you can change immediately?
3. Share your findings with all the necessary stakeholders; this is likely to include the learner, their parents, their tutor (if secondary) and the SENCo. Consider how active a role they should take.

There is no need to mention or assign any labels at this point. Just identify the specific need and take small steps to address it. In Chapter 7 there are several ideas for you to try in relation to supporting learning in the classroom.

THE MAIN THING IS YOU ARE AWARE AND OPEN TO CHANGING YOUR APPROACH TO MEET THEIR NEEDS.

Your Worldview of Special Educational Needs and Disability

If your understanding of SEND is not informed by personal experience, you might rely on anecdotal information such as buff coloured paper for dyslexic learners or a visual timetable for an autistic learner. They both have their merits but will not work for everyone and can result in a limited approach to addressing the needs of those with challenges in the classroom.

As a SENCo, I often advocated for all classrooms to have a SEND toolkit. This would include reading rulers, pencil grips, number lines, key vocabulary, homophones and commonly misspelt words, reading windows and Post-It notes. Whilst this approach will not meet the specific needs of some children, it may facilitate an independent approach to learning and scaffold some activities.

Moment of Reflection 1.8: Curiosity

Consider for two minutes what you might think are some disadvantages of the SEND toolkit.

As I now reflect on such recommendations as a systems thinker, I see several disadvantages to such an approach and how this well-meaning strategy can lead to further problems which then cloud the intended purpose.

The potential difficulties are:

1. Learners don't feel comfortable with leaving their seat to collect their resources.
2. There is a stigma around using the resources.
3. They haven't been shown the resources or how to use them.

4. They don't know what they need without further support or discussion.
5. They don't know if they're eligible to use the resource.

If, as a SENCo, I had taken a broader perspective on recommending SEND toolkits to teacher, I would have ensured that the kits were available to all and that the resources were explained and linked to particular tasks. For example, if a learner needs to do lots of reading, a reading ruler might help. Or starting a new piece of writing, a framework for writing might help get them started. The kit then becomes an exploration of different ways of working which happen to include scaffolds for learning difficulties rather than a SEND toolkit which both isolates and excludes learners at the same time.

In the first of a series of practitioner letters, Gemma Archer explains her approach to teaching and how systems thinking has developed her practice. She is an assistant headteacher and International Baccalaureate Diploma Programme coordinator.

Dear practitioner,

Over the years, I've had the opportunity to practice and refine my teaching and leadership in different international school settings. Yet, despite all the fine-tuning and adapting, I noticed a recurring pattern: the same issues and frustrations kept surfacing each year. I was adjusting lessons and implementing new strategies, but it often felt like I was addressing symptoms rather than root causes. Systems thinking helped me step back and see these complexities from a new perspective.

In terms of leadership, adopting a systems thinking mindset meant becoming more reflexive. I began to regularly examine my beliefs and assumptions about teaching and leadership, questioning how my actions might influence not just individual students and teachers but also the entire classroom environment and the school's broader culture. This realisation was both empowering and humbling. On the one hand, it empowered me to influence change more holistically. On the other hand, it humbled me to see that some of my well-intentioned efforts had unintended consequences.

There were times when my interventions didn't have the impact I expected, prompting me to reflect deeply on what might have gone wrong and why. Systems thinking taught me to view these moments not as failures but as part of a continuous learning cycle – opportunities to reflect, adapt, and evolve my practice by looking again at what else was interacting with the system I had intervened in. Through this ongoing process of self-reflection, I've learned to adapt my approaches more thoughtfully, being mindful of how my actions align with my intentions and their broader impact.

One of the most valuable insights systems thinking offered was understanding the concept of time lag and the importance of looking beyond immediate solutions. Early in my career, I believed that if a student struggled, the remedy had to be quick and direct. It was frustrating when changes didn't lead to immediate or sustained improvements. Systems thinking shifted my perspective. Instead of asking, 'How do I fix this now?' I began asking, 'What patterns have led us here?' By seeking feedback from students and parents and examining these recurring patterns, I started to see struggles in a new light. It became less about short-term fixes and more about fostering an environment where we could address root causes. I began using the readily available data to iterate and refine our curriculum in ways that supported longer-term student growth, focusing on what was within my circle of influence. This shift wasn't always comfortable, but it created space for more meaningful progress in our context.

As a Geographer in the classroom, systems thinking also changed my approach to planning and differentiation. I always aimed to scaffold tasks but hadn't fully considered how interconnected these steps were. To support this, I began using diagrams and graphic organisers more systematically. These tools helped students visually organise information, reducing the sense of overwhelm when faced with challenging tasks. They acted as mental scaffolds, providing different ways to process and make sense of complex or abstract concepts. As students became more confident using these strategies, I gradually removed the supports. There were moments of discomfort for me and the students, especially when the safety nets were lifted. Yet, this was where the real growth occurred. Students began to develop their methods for organising information, able to increasingly manage their mindset and build the resilience and independence needed for deeper learning.

What systems thinking has given me, above all, is a mindset that values complexity, ambiguity and the importance of incorporating alternative perspectives. It's not about having the perfect answer or being in control. It's about being curious, reflective and open to the idea that learning – ours and our students – is an ongoing process. By embracing this mindset, I've found a greater sense of purpose and patience in my practice.

I wish you all the best as you navigate your own systems thinking journey in education.

Warmly,

Gemma

Applying Systems Thinking to Develop a System for Support

Up to this point, we have explored the foundations of systems thinking: interrelationships, boundary judgements and interconnectivity. It is also understood that systems thinking requires flexibility and an ability to embrace uncertainty. The benefit of systems thinking is that it puts such ideas into practice and has developed several tools in order to explore these things and to enable a person to make sense of tricky, messy and often wicked problems. A wicked problem (Rittel & Webber, 1973) is used to describe a social or cultural issue which is seemingly impossible to resolve. They have no single solution and are persistent in nature. They typically involve multiple stakeholders making a consensus hard to achieve with solutions offering quick fixes and often more problems down the line.

The following models are intended to provide an individual or a group with tools to explore ideas and to take a reflective look at your classroom, subject or setting.

The first step in the system thinking process is to identify the approach. It is encouraged over the course of this book that you attempt all stages outlined in this diagram and there will be recommendations for how to follow each step of the diagram as the book progresses.

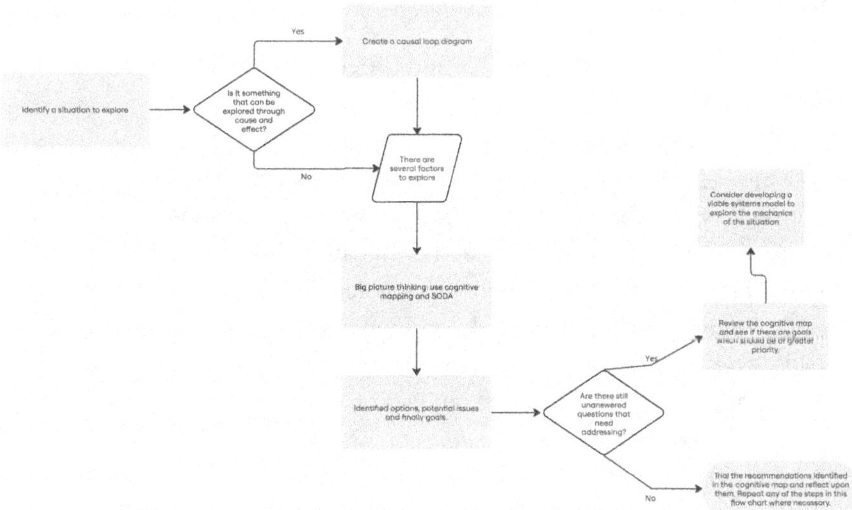

Figure 1.5 A flowchart to aid problem solving

A situation to begin with might be to support a diverse range of needs in a classroom.

This is a suggested order in which the following models can be implemented, and the following chapters outline the areas of practice which might benefit from such an approach.

Causal Loop Diagrams

The first tool that is to be introduced is intended to provide a way to measure the impact of something on a system. Whilst you can create a causal loop diagram (CLD) when exploring a situation, sometimes it's useful to do so on paper first. There are also websites which create a loop diagram for you. The advantage of using technology to create the causal loop is that you can see which areas of the loop are being visited the most and this helps in the decision making that should follow a CLD. An example of this can be found below:

Causal loop diagrams:

- are concise and visual
- reveal the interconnections both obvious and hidden
- can be used to elicit and capture the mental models of individuals or teams
- can expand the boundary of people's thinking beyond the familiar parameters
- can help identify commonalities and provide the impetus to discuss differences.

A CLD consists of a set of **nodes**, which represent **variables** in the system, and arrows, which represent the causal relationships between the variables. The arrows can have either a positive or negative sign, which indicates whether the relationship is reinforcing or balancing.

A reinforcing loop is a feedback loop in which the change in one variable leads to a change in another variable, which in turn leads to a further change in the first variable, and so on. This type of loop can lead to exponential growth or decline, depending on the signs of the arrows.

A reinforcing loop shows how if a person continues to have time to develop their level of education, this will lead to growth which will continue throughout the cycle and keep being reinforced. Conversely, if

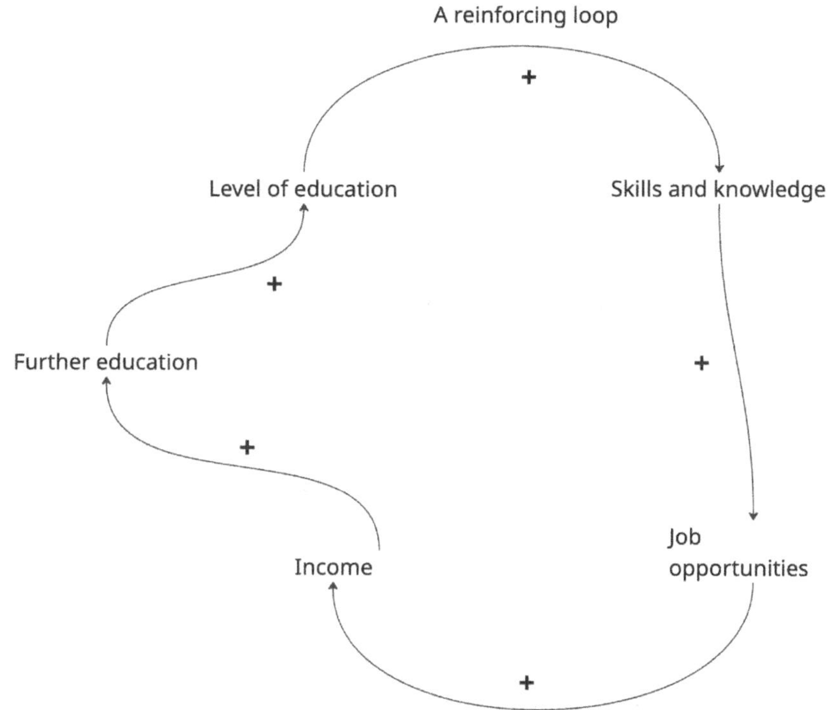

Figure 1.6 A reinforcing loop (contains an even number – including zero – of negative links)

there is an imbalance at any point in the loop, for example an identified skills gap, this will lead to fewer job opportunities, less money, less investment in education and so on. A reinforcing loop amplifies change.

A balancing loop is a system structure that tries to maintain stability. When something goes too high or too low the loop pushes back to keep things in balance. The example below explains the link between spelling and vocabulary. Spelling errors increase and an intervention to improve a learner's vocabulary is implemented, and as a result there is an increase in vocabulary knowledge which in term improves spelling accuracy and spelling errors decrease. If they are seen to increase again, the loop responds, and the circuit starts again.

Of course, the real world is more complex than this simple CLD. There are many other factors that can affect education, economic prosperity and social mobility. However, this CLD can help us to understand some of the key causal relationships between these variables.

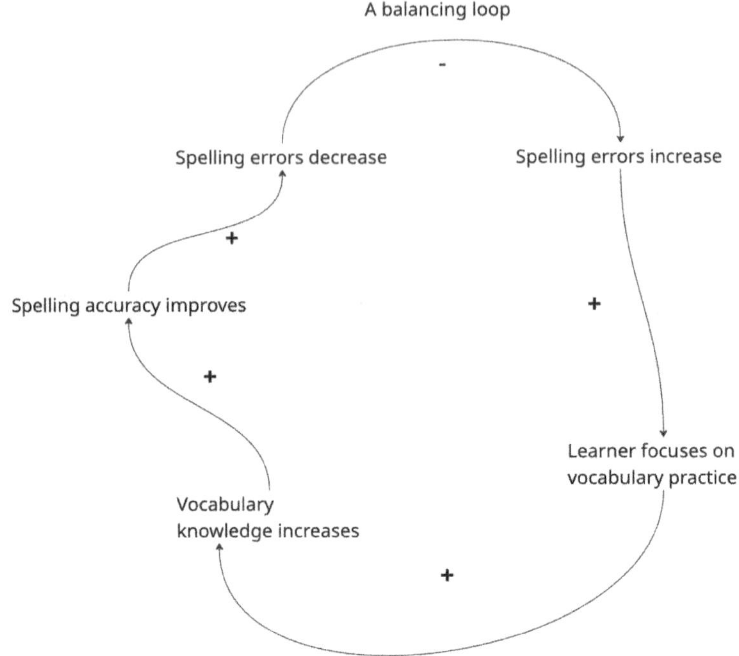

Figure 1.7 A balancing loop (contains an odd number of negative links)

CLDs can be a useful tool for understanding complex systems. They can help us identify the key variables in a system, the causal relationships between these variables, and the feedback loops that can lead to either growth or decline. This can help us to develop more effective policies and interventions to improve the system.

General guidance for creating a CDL is:

1. To keep the names of the variables snappy, avoid using verbs. The nouns can have adjectives and should imply some way of measurement.
2. The arrows have meaning, consider their direction and what happens if this direction is reversed. They act as the first indicator of feedback whether positive or negative.
3. Use curved lines; this not only looks more appealing but is easier to follow.
4. Important loops should follow circular or oval paths, but it might not be obvious at the start which are the important loops so take time to iterate.

5. Minimise crossed lines. Try to spread out the diagram if you can.
6. Keep it clean – I'm not talking language here. Make it as easy to read as possible.
7. Iterate, don't expect to nail it on the first go. One of the most liberating factors about systems thinking is t iteration.
8. When you are pleased with it, recreate it on loopy.com where it will come to life for you and can show you any areas of congestion or broken links.

Moment for Reflection 1.9: Interrelationships

Now it's your turn to give this a go. Consider an intervention which you have recently introduced into your classroom and plot it on a CLD. Is it having the desired impact you hoped? Are there other side effects that you didn't anticipate?

When you start to think of systems, it's impossible not to see them everywhere. Below is an example of a school system and within each section there will be a hierarchy or a system which can be autonomous for the most part, but will require different levels of engagement with other parts of the system at times.

Moment of Reflection 1.10: Curiosity

Take a moment to reflect upon this image and consider your role in the system:

- What contribution do you make?
- How are you impacted by this system?
- What is in your control and what is not?
- What are the boundary judgements?

CLD is helpful to explore cause and effect but when you want to delve a little deeper you need a tool from systems thinking which enables a broader view and can start to tackle the complexity of a situation.

Figure 1.8 The different levels of influence in a school

Cognitive Mapping – Thinking of Absolutely Everything Then Taking a Step Back

Cognitive mapping is a technique used to represent a person's (or a group's) mental model of a particular process or concept. It is a visual representation of how someone understands something and can be used to understand how people think about a problem, make decisions or solve problems.

Cognitive maps can be used in a variety of situations:

- User research: To understand how someone thinks about an intervention or a topic.
- Problem solving: To identify the key elements of a problem and the relationships between them.
- Decision making: To explore the different options available and their potential consequences.

- Conflict resolution: To identify the different perspectives on a conflict and the potential solutions.
- Strategy development: To map out the different steps involved in achieving a goal.

Each one of these could be really useful in the classroom. Consider the following examples:

Table 1.2 Ways to use cognitive mapping in the classroom

User Research	Your setting is considering options for after school clubs
Problem Solving	You have noticed a dip in comprehension in your learners
Decision Making	Whether to carry out a formative or summative assessment at the end of a topic
Conflict Resolution	A fall out regarding a seating plan continues to disrupt lessons
Strategy Development	A whole school focus on reading has been implemented; how do you ensure it is evident in your medium- and long-term planning?

Cognitive maps can be created in a variety of ways, but they typically involve the following steps:

1. Identifying the key concepts or elements of the process or concept being mapped.
2. Determining the relationships between the concepts.
3. Representing the concepts and relationships visually.

The visual representation of a cognitive map can take many forms, such as a flowchart, a mind map, or a network diagram. The best format for a particular cognitive map will depend on the purpose of the map and the preferences of the person creating it.

Cognitive mapping is a powerful tool for understanding how people think about the world. It can be used to improve communication, problem solving and decision making. It would be a useful exercise at the beginning of a new academic year to get to know a class and its motivations / likes and dislikes as well as their specific learning needs.

Here are some of the benefits of using cognitive mapping:

- It can help to identify the key concepts and relationships in a complex problem.
- It can help to visualise the different options available and their potential consequences.
- It can help to facilitate communication and collaboration between different people.
- It can help to identify potential solutions to problems.
- It can help to improve decision-making processes.

It is most often a collaborative exercise, but the example in the following section can also be done as an individual.

Moment of Reflection 1.11: Multiple Perspectives

What opportunity might you have as a group to explore a topic using a cognitive map?
What value might this bring to the discussion?

Cognitive Mapping: Strategic Options Development Analysis Model (Ackermann & Eden, 2010)

Strategic Options Development and Analysis (SODA) is a problem-structuring method that helps organisations and individuals to identify and evaluate strategic options. It is a qualitative approach that uses cognitive mapping to capture the different perspectives of stakeholders and to explore the relationships between different factors.

SODA is a four-step process:

1. Problem structuring: The first step is to identify the problem or issue that the organisation is facing. This is done by gathering information from stakeholders and by using cognitive mapping to represent the different perspectives on the problem. The best way to do this is with Post-It notes or index cards and writing out as many as possible. There should be no attempt, at this stage, to order them.

2. Options generation: The second step is to generate a list of potential strategic options. This is in response to the problems/issues which were generated in step 1. Hopefully some clusters of information will develop, and you can start to group the Post-It notes in some way. This can be done by brainstorming, by using checklists, or by using other creativity techniques.
3. Strategic directions: The third step is to evaluate the different strategic options. Imagine step 2 will be at the classroom level but many of the options you have identified might require finance or outside agencies or resourcing. This will set them apart from those options which are under your control. It might also make them less of a priority for you.
4. Decision making: The fourth step is to make a decision about which strategic option to pursue. This decision is made by considering the results of the evaluation and by taking into account the preferences of the stakeholders. It recognises that whilst we all intend to do everything we can in our settings, we need to be strategic about our choices, and SODA mapping provides that big-picture thinking but identifies a set of manageable and hopefully attainable goals by the end of the process.

SODA is a flexible and adaptable approach that can be used to address a wide range of strategic problems. It is particularly useful for problems that are complex or that involve a lot of uncertainty. This version is simplified and has been adapted for both individual use and uses the principles of SODA rather than adhering strictly to the model. An example and further explanation of SODA is provided in Chapter 3.

Moment of Reflection 1.12: Interrelationships

I would recommend returning to SODA mapping at the end of the book as there will be several strategy options presented over the next few chapters which you might want to consider. However, you might want to spend a few minutes reflecting on a class or group of students and identify some of the issues/problems you and they may face. These will provide you with the basis of a SODA map which you can then develop at a later date.

The final and perhaps most comprehensive model of systems thinking which I would like to introduce you to is called the viable systems model which at first glance looks complicated and time consuming, but I have used it for several different projects including a good look at myself and my personal life. It is intended to be adapted and changed rather than being a definitive representation of a situation.

The Viable Systems Model

The viable systems model (VSM; Espejo, 1990) is a systems thinking model that describes the essential elements and functions of any viable system, which is a system that can survive and adapt in a changing environment. The VSM was developed by Stafford Beer in the 1970s and has been used to understand and improve the functioning of organisations, governments and other systems.

The VSM consists of five interconnected systems:

- System 1: The operational system, which is responsible for the day-to-day activities.
- System 2: The coordination system, which ensures that the different parts of the organisation are working together effectively.
- System 3: The control system, which monitors the environment and makes adjustments to the organisation's activities as needed.
- System 4: The intelligence system, which scans the environment for opportunities and threats.
- System 5: The policy system, which sets the organisation's overall goals and strategy.

The VSM can be used to diagnose and improve the functioning of any system by identifying strengths and weaknesses in each of the five systems. It can also be used to design new systems or to make changes to existing systems.

The VSM is based on the following principles:

- **Requisite variety:** A system must have the capacity to match the variety of its environment in order to survive. For example, if learners require more support with a specific topic than has been considered in the planning, the teaching of these individuals may result in delays or a breakdown in communication. The knock-on effect may be seen in other areas of the system if the lack of requisite variety is not reflected upon.

- **Equifinality:** There are many different ways for a system to achieve its goals. This reflects the need for curiosity and a flexible approach to support. Hold any strategy lightly as what works for one cohort may not for another.
- **Autonomy:** A system must be able to regulate itself in order to maintain its viability. This is the responsibility of system 2 and 3 and requires the checks and balances in a school to work efficiently in order for teaching and learning to progress without much consideration of those checks and balances. Safeguarding procedures are an example of this.
- **Emergence:** The properties of a system emerge from the interaction of its parts. This is perhaps the most important aspect of this model as it enables you to see where communication may be falling short or there is a mismatch between the intention of the message and how it is received. It can also show you if any parts of the systems are taking too much energy or time and adversely impacting other parts of the system. Working your way through this book will hopefully allow space and time for strategies and ideas to emerge. It is difficult to resist problem solving but sometimes the right path is only clear when you've started walking.

The VSM diagram shared not only provides you with an outline to follow in creating your own system but it also demonstrates how this book was built with the chapters informing each part of the system. You can build each section of your own VSM as you go along by using pencil and paper or a virtual whiteboard.

System 1: This is related to what you do and is the factory floor of the model. It is the operational tasks and can include both classroom tasks as well as personal life.

Common issues within this system are a breakdown in communication, a lack of requisite variety leading to burnout, overwhelm or getting behind with tasks.

It can be limited due to the communication and information provided to and by system 2 as well as system 3 not being robust enough to handle all the operations in system 1.

System 2: This system is all about communication and is informed both by system 1 and 3. It could include a variety of different ways of communicating and involve lots of different stakeholders. What and how this information is shared will be different from one education setting to another but is likely to include assessment information, pastoral and progress, as well as school, departmental and parental communication.

Issues which might arise from this system include misunderstandings, inflexible timetables or schedules, communication channels which are ineffective, and siloed departments with little opportunity for interaction.

System 3: Resourcing and planning are the role of this system, and again it can be informed and inform systems 1, 3 and 4. It needs to be able to assimilate the directives from system 4 in order for the practitioner to apply it to an operational setting. When system 3 works well it is resourced and informed, providing flexible and current strategies to support learning. When it does not work so well it is often as a result of top-down instruction which is not monitored. There is a disproportionate amount of bureaucracy which is not supported by the communication system or is having a negative impact on the operational system. It can also be responsible for resource mismanagement.

System 4: This system is forward thinking and future planning. It has its sights on the horizon and is scanning for new opportunities, new ways of thinking. The planning which takes place in this system is long term. It synthesises both information from the environment and also system 5 in order to resource and inform system 3 in preparation for implementation. This system can experience problems if it does not embrace new ways of working or is not scanning the horizon effectively for changes in the environment. It may be passive and reluctant to change. Or can chase every shiny new strategy without giving it time to settle and embed into the setting.

System 5: The vision and values of the education setting are system 5. They can be informed by the environment including the local community and will be responsible for overall governance. It can become an issue if there is a misalignment between policy and practice. Changes to working practices which are governed by political changes or a lack of consistent leadership.

When you reach the end of the book, there are some questions for you to consider identifying which areas of the system are having the most influence on your practice and whether there is an imbalance in the system which needs addressing. This model is easier to understand when you see it and have a play around with it.

To conclude this chapter, applying the ideas of interrelationships, multiple perspectives and boundary judgements will foster an open and fair practice that is better equipped to deal with uncertainty and complexity. It is more agile and reflective rather than being fixed or rigid which enables a greater degree of flexibility to meet the needs of learners in the classroom. It recognises the importance of self-reflection, sensitivity and consideration

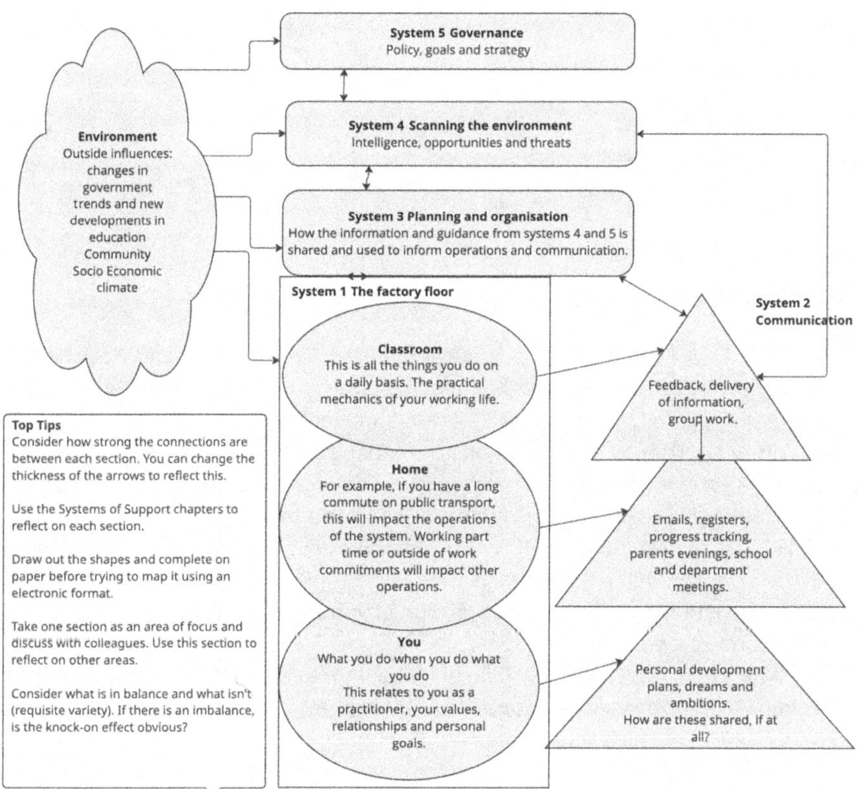

Figure 1.9 The VSM relating to this book and to education settings

for all the stakeholders, including both the learners and you as the practitioner.

If your interest in systems thinking is piqued, I highly recommend the short course on it available through Open Learn (see www.open.edu/openlearn/science-maths-technology/mastering-systems-thinking-practice).

Moments of Reflection

- 1.1 Interrelationships
- 1.2 Practice
- 1.3 Interrelationships
- 1.4 Practice
- 1.5 Curiosity
- 1.6 Curiosity
- 1.7 Multiple Perspectives
- 1.8 Curiosity
- 1.9 Interrelationships
- 1.10 Curiosity
- 1.11 Multiple Perspectives
- 1.12 Interrelationships

References

Ackermann, F., & Eden, C. (2010). Strategic Options Development and Analysis. In M. Reynolds & S. Holwell (Eds), *Systems approached to making change: A practical guide* (2nd ed., pp. 139–200). Springer-Verlag.

Education Act. (2011). www.legislation.gov.uk/ukpga/2011/21/contents

Espejo, R. (1990). *Viable systems model*. www.researchgate.net/publication/225863384_The_Viable_System_Model

Rittel, H. W. J., & Webber, M. M. (1973). Dilemmas in a general theory of planning. *Policy Sciences*, *4*(2), 155–169.

SEND Code of Practice. (2014). www.gov.uk/government/publications/send-code-of-practice-0-to-25

United Nations. (n.d.). Goals: 13. Take urgent action to combat climate change and its impacts. https://sdgs.un.org/goals/goal13#targets_and_indicators

2
The Education Landscape

Overview

Understanding the education landscape is essential for creating a frame of reference. It encourages curiosity about what can be achieved at the same time as acceptance that some things are out of your control. This chapter will provide you with ideas of what to add to the environment section of the VSM. It will also begin work on the most productive element of the VSM, system 1. It is the part of the system informed by action and influenced by all the other parts of the system. It can be easily overwhelmed and cause imbalances.

This chapter starts with you, your values, reflections and perspectives. It then considers the development of SEND practices, before moving on to consider the barriers to learning. These establish boundary judgements which are always being made when working with people. At the end of this chapter, you will have a clear idea of your own boundary judgements in regard to your practice, setting and learners.

As explained in chapter 1, a key approach in systems thinking is the ability to consider your own part in the system which you are trying to change. This is deeper than reflection which most in education are familiar with even on the surface level of reflecting whether a lesson went well or not.

In order to consider what you are bringing to the system you first need to reflect upon your own experiences and perspectives.

DOI: 10.4324/9781003400639-3

Moment of Reflection 2.1: Curiosity

Take a few minutes to reflect on your education considering the difference between primary and secondary.

How did you build the foundations of basic skills such as numeracy and literacy? Can you recall individual practitioners, what impact did they have on you?

Now consider the value the education setting placed on grades.

Did this motivate or dishearten you?

What support was there for your aspirations?

How, if at all, did this inform your values?

There are also other factors which will impact that learner's trajectory through education and a practitioner's perception of those learners is one of them. No one is without bias as experiences shape how we see the world. The key is to be able to recognise these biases and address them with curiosity and compassion.

Moment of Reflection 2.2: Multiple Perspectives

Take a moment to consider these preconceptions related to autism, ADHD and dyslexia which may or may not form part of your perspective. Then consider how this preconception may influence how you plan tasks for these learners or respond to their needs in the classroom.

- Autism – does not give eye contact.
- ADHD – needs movement breaks every ten minutes.
- Dyslexia – needs all worksheets printed on buff paper.

Values-Driven Practice

A crucial element of this approach is an understanding of what you bring as a person to the classroom; not your education, or even your experience, but your personal values. Do not think too deeply and select a top ten. Once you have your top ten, narrow it down to five before deciding upon two. Then think about how these values might influence your teaching.

Table 2.1 A list of 50 possible values

integrity	*authenticity*	*growth*	*optimism*	*altruism*
honesty	courage	perseverance	determination	independence
kindness	gratitude	service	innovation	equality
compassion	humility	connection	self-discipline	mindfulness
respect	empathy	joy	excellence	adventure
responsibility	accountability	balance	patience	success
fairness	wisdom	learning	community	diversity
trust	justice	open-mindedness	health	spirituality
loyalty	freedom	peace	fun	self-respect
love	creativity	security	generosity	purpose

Moment of Reflection 2.3: Interrelationships

If you shared these with your class, would they choose the same values for you?

Are you demonstrating other values which you are perhaps unaware of?

Being aware of your values is the starting point to analysing your performance in the classroom. Once you have these values in place and you've considered how visible they are in your practice, the next step is to consider your values in relation to your own experience of an education setting. This can evoke strong emotions so be kind to yourself.

Moment of Reflection 2.4: Practice

Write down your values and list them alongside your current accommodations for those with additional learning needs. Is there any crossover? Could you align your values more closely to your practice? What are your current strategies to get to know your learners? Do they rely on one particular mode of communication over another?

SEND Is the Lens but Not the Only Perspective

Consider SEND the lens through which this book explores challenges in the classroom. This could apply to other marginalised groups, as the feeling that the system was not built for a certain group of people is felt by many. SEND can have a profound impact in a classroom, and how it is recognised and addressed can leave a lasting impression on a learner.

Whilst this book has chosen to consider the experience of learners with SEND as the primary focus, it does not intend to separate or prioritise their needs from others that may find it challenging to access the curriculum. Many learners in education will experience highs and lows; there is a cohort for which every day can be a challenge. Some learners flourish from their first day in nursery whilst others will leave at 18 or 19 having never found their groove. There are those who try so hard they burn out due to their effort to keep up, and there are those who choose to fail rather than own up to their struggles. Some will be nurtured by a practitioner and suddenly things turn round for them, whilst others experience practitioners who don't understand them, and this will impact the rest of their educational experience.

These are learning-based challenges; you then also have home life, social life, emotional development, and mental and physical health challenges. Growing up is a time of so much change and it overwhelms even the most resilient of learners at times.

Giving consideration, from the outset, of shared language in a setting can highlight the understanding of inclusion of the staff and identify any gaps in knowledge. It can identify the setting's starting point in relation to inclusive language and where it should place its focus for further training. Let's first begin by thinking about the language used for SEND and learning difficulties.

Figure 2.1 A word cloud of several words relating to SEND

Most of these words suggest that the problem lies with the learner and that they need something different from the rest of their peers in order to learn. This implies that the rest are normal, and all learn the same way. It also implies more work for the practitioner in order to meet the needs of these learners, and this can be too much for some practitioners.

A move away from blaming one element of a system, be that a person, resource or way of working, is encouraged as such an approach is limiting. When that one element is a learner or young person, they will quickly feel like they are the problem, which can lead to a lack of self-confidence, apathy and a limiting of what they believe they can achieve.

Moment of Reflection 2.5: Multiple Perspectives

What is the status of SEND in your setting? Is there a shared language about SEND, and how positive is it?

Laura Dobson is an experienced and knowledgeable leader who is passionate about supporting learners to develop a love of learning. Her specialisms include literacy, assessment, moderation and developing an inclusive culture in an education setting. She is currently a deputy headteacher at a large primary education setting, and has previously been a regional teaching and learning advisor.

Dear reader,

It's 2024, and in recent years our knowledge about neurodiversity has developed at a rate of knots.

A friend working for a large multinational company asked me this week why education settings weren't doing more to accommodate neurodiversity when businesses do so much.

I found the comment disheartening as I see the sheer hard work that goes on in education settings to allow ALL learners to thrive. But, ultimately, for some learners, the classroom setting is far from ideal. I, for one, could never work in an open-plan office, which ultimately is what a classroom is. In order to work effectively, I need silence, which might be at odds with my classmate who needs to hum and fiddle in order to focus.

Sadly, in education settings, we don't have the luxury (or money) to accommodate home working, flexible start times, private offices, mentors and so on.

So how can practitioners make the classroom and its fairly rigid framework as inclusive as possible?

1) *Listen to the learner. Learners need to feel heard. Find out what they find works for them and discuss ways this can be implemented in the classroom. Rest breaks, movement breaks, being close to a window or sitting at the back of the class – these are all small adjustments that make a big difference.*
2) *Educate learners on differences so they understand that our brains work differently and that is great. There are some excellent story books that can facilitate that discussion.*
3) *Utilise technology.*
4) *Find and praise the good. Hold learners in mind and comment on their strengths.*
5) *Ensure a rigorous mental health programme. Self-esteem is an important consideration for all learners. If a practitioner notices this is dropping, what emotional support can be given?*
6) *Task design – walk through a lesson in somebody's shoes and consider if further scaffolding is required.*

From Laura Dobson,

Deputy Headteacher

Moment of Reflection 2.6: Practice

What are your greatest challenges in the classroom when supporting learners?

Spend two minutes writing down everything that comes to mind; this might include challenges for the learners, but also challenges for you as a practitioner and challenges for the education setting. Try not to limit your answers to any particular thing and try to keep writing to allow space for your feelings and deeper held beliefs to surface too.

Keep these reflections as they will be useful later in the book when you start to consider your system of support in more depth.

Whilst an awareness of the system and its functions is important, at times, use of that system to support the progress of some learners is required. It is important to understand its limitations and not apply or use the systems to reduce learners to simply the sum of their difficulties.

In the first chapter, the ways in which systems thinking can foster a holistic approach to support were considered. This chapter, whilst exploring the SEND landscape, will now look to apply some of those strategies to achieve the following:

1. Develop an awareness of your own understanding of SEND.
2. Identify the limitations of the current system.
3. Understand SEND in its current iteration.
4. Appreciate the progress made to date on social understanding and acceptance of SEND.
5. Outline what you might change/adapt as a result of your reflections during this chapter.

The intention, from the outset, is to support action and there will be opportunities throughout the book to reflect on your current practice and ideas and suggestions on how to adapt your practice to support individual needs in the classroom.

It would be a reduced perspective not to consider the changing nature of education settings and consider the complex and changing nature of education which frames every practitioner's role and actions. The overarching education system is inextricably linked to the political climate and the economy. Some changes to the system are significant but the structure of education settings has not changed significantly since compulsory education was introduced in 1880.

The Focus on Competition and Achievement

The English education system is highly competitive, and learners are constantly being assessed and ranked. This emphasis on competition can lead to stress and anxiety, and it can also reinforce the idea that success is only achieved through individual effort. This has made its way from GCSEs to primary education with the introduction of SATs in 1991 and then even earlier in a child's education with the Year 1 phonics check (in 2012). Whilst assessment can identify areas to work on and national trends in performance, one of the consequences can be additional stress for learners. Education settings have found ways to reduce this stress for the learners, and assessments and tests have always been a part of education settings. However, this assessment data is also used for the school's benefit too. Consider how this dual purpose for assessment can impact the process. What happens if the intended outcome is to improve a school's exam performance rather than support individual performance? How does the approach change? What impact would this have on the delivery of the assessment and the reporting of the results?

Tom Richmond (2021) argues that GCSEs are now defunct due to the compulsory education setting leaving age being set at 19: 'As pupils in England are required to be in some form of education and training up to the age of 18, it is reasonable to conclude that the current approach of setting 'education setting-leaving qualifications' at age 16 is no longer required'.

A focus on summative assessment and a reduction of options to study more coursework-based courses has limited the options for learners, in particular those that find traditional studying with an exam at the end difficult.

Competition and Achievement

If the measure of competence does not take into account individual differences, some learners with SEND will always be considered behind or, worse still, failing. If they are to be measured against a national framework, they will never be able to compete or achieve. However, this binary approach, all or nothing, does not represent the breadth of skills which all learners have, and therefore there needs to be flexibility in the approach.

The Focus Is on Traditional Subjects

The English education curriculum is still heavily focused on core subjects, such as maths, science and English. This has led to a narrowing of the curriculum in many education settings, especially when combined with the requirement that all learners must leave an education setting with a maths and English GCSE pass (level 4). Functional numerical and literacy skills are an absolute must, but the delivery and the assessment of such skills remains old-fashioned and selective. It favours those with good memories, fast recall, decoding skills and language awareness. This means that many with dyslexia, dyscalculia and language difficulties will struggle to demonstrate their knowledge of these subjects due to their difficulties with the secretarial skills required to record their answers.

Lessons from Alternative Provisions

It is reasonable to surmise that a learner arriving at an alternative provision (AP) will have developed a negative opinion of education settings and learning. They are highly likely to have learning difficulties (24.2% of all learners in AP have an Education, Health and Care Plan and 58.1% require SEND support (Department of Education, 2023/24), which will have made the classroom a challenging place to be. One of the first and perhaps most important challenges in AP is to gain the learner's trust and begin to introduce them to the joys of learning once again. I have never met a learner devoid of curiosity, but a learner has to feel at ease, safe and capable. They are likely to have missed elements of the curriculum in their mainstream setting and could have missed key learning concepts which will make building on their knowledge difficult. There is a significant possibility that they have sat in lessons which make little sense to them, and the level of work has been inaccessible.

In an AP, the curriculum can be set and followed but there is the added complication of a small time frame in which to support the learner, as short as 12 weeks. This makes the choice of what to teach these learners crucial. Whilst one education setting might place the emphasis on reading using whole class readers or creating a library and using posters to inspire a love of words, another might focus on being prepared to learn, including aspects of mindfulness and metacognition to ensure the learners are ready to learn.

What I learned from spending time working with APs is the commitment to the learner as an individual and the staff's belief in that learner and what they can achieve. This is not possible without spending time building a secure, trusting relationship.

Moment of Reflection 2.7: Boundary Judgement

If you have a learner that is at risk of being excluded or moving to another provision, what do you have in place as an individual or as an education setting to support this transition? Similarly, if your education setting has a new starter who has been moved from another education setting mid-term, what do you have in place to ease and support that transition?

Equality and Diversity

> The daily attitudes your people bring with them as they walk through your education setting gates and the decisions they make will impact on everyone.
>
> *Nic Ponsford, founder of Global Equality Collective (2023)*

An education setting becomes its own community with leaders, role models and spokespeople. Learners grow and develop their own ways of working through learning in the classroom and the playground or in their social groups. Sometimes, who learners surround themselves with can have a greater impact, particularly in the teenage years, than their own families. Siblings can follow very different paths depending on their cohort: one might continue to study and the other might leave education and seek work. A friend of mine always comments that it was because all her friends went to university that she did too.

Returning to Ponsford's quote, there is great value in recognising the identities and diversity in an education community and making adapting to differences common practice, not a special event or one-off activity.

There are many reasons why practitioners should know more about equality and diversity in an education setting. Here are a few:

- To create a safe and inclusive learning environment. When practitioners have a good understanding of equality and diversity, they are better able to create a classroom environment where learners feel safe and respected.
- To challenge stereotypes and biases. Practitioners can play a vital role in challenging stereotypes and biases that learners may have. By teaching learners about different cultures and perspectives, practitioners can help them to develop a more open and inclusive mindset.
- To prepare learners for the real world. In today's globalised world, it is more important than ever for learners to be prepared to interact with people from diverse backgrounds. Practitioners can help learners to develop the skills and knowledge they need to succeed in a multicultural society by teaching them about equality and diversity.

Here are some specific examples of how practitioners can use their knowledge of equality and diversity to support learning:

- Use inclusive language and imagery. Practitioners can be mindful of the language and imagery they use in their classrooms to ensure that it is inclusive of all learners. For example, instead of using specific terms like 'man' or 'boy', practitioners can use more generic terms like 'person' or 'learner'.
- Teach about different cultures and perspectives. Practitioners can incorporate lessons about different cultures and perspectives into their curriculum.
- Challenge stereotypes and biases. When practitioners see learners engaging in stereotypical or biased behaviour, they can gently challenge them and help them to see things from a different perspective.

If you're interested in finding out more about equality and diversity do consider looking at the work of the Global Equality Collective (www.thegec.education). Increasing awareness and understanding of both diversity and learning differences will lead to increased tolerance and hopefully society can learn from the examples set by our young people.

This letter is from Bigi Luetchford, a parenting coach who helps parents move beyond traditional roles and power struggles – raising children with empathy and respect no matter what their family looks like.

Moment of Reflection 2.8: Interrelationships and Boundary Judgement

As you read Bigi's letter, consider your own beliefs and knowledge regarding individual differences and how you respect them in the classroom. What if the new addition to your classroom had been previously educated at home or moved mid-term to your setting – how might you approach their settling-in and what strategies might you use to enable them to become comfortable with what could be an unsettling environment for them?

Dear practitioner,

Embracing curiosity, fostering relationships with parents and learning from an education setting.

It's time we saw learners as the whole individuals that they are, instead of incomplete humans who need to be moulded into the right shape. Each one is beautifully unique and worthy of being celebrated!

In my work as a parenting coach, I've seen how easily assumptions can shape interactions, often unintentionally. As a neurodivergent individual and the parent of a neurodivergent teenager, I know first-hand how frustrating it can be when others assume they understand your needs or challenges before truly listening. This experience has taught me the importance of leading with curiosity rather than judgement. In any educational setting, it's vital to remain open, asking questions like, 'What might this learner be trying to communicate?' or 'What haven't I considered yet?' Approaching each learner with a mindset of discovery not only allows practitioners to see beyond labels but also to build stronger, more empathetic connections with those they teach.

My coaching practice also emphasises the importance of collaboration between parents and practitioners, particularly when supporting learners with SEND, LGBTQ+ families or non-traditional structures like solo parents and blended families. Practitioners can foster positive relationships by prioritising open, needs-based communication and empathy. This means actively listening to parents' concerns, validating their perspectives, and focusing on the underlying needs of both the learner and the family. By maintaining an open dialogue, an education setting can create an atmosphere of trust and mutual respect, making it easier to address challenges together. This approach helps ensure that parents feel heard and valued, which can lead to more effective support for learners' well-being and growth, even within the education settings' limited resources.

As someone who embraces the philosophy of an education setting and values self-directed learning, I see the transformative potential of giving learners more agency in their education. My son has thrived in an environment where he can pursue his interests and learn at his own pace. An education setting is not about abandoning structure but about recognising that learning happens best when it's driven by curiosity. Traditional practitioners can integrate this philosophy by offering more choices, encouraging learners to follow their passions, and creating spaces where learners' voices are valued. When we shift from a rigid curriculum to a more collaborative, learner-centred approach, we give young people the freedom to truly thrive.

Wishing Kelly, practitioners, parents and carers, and all young people all the best!

Bigi Luetchford, Parenting Coach

Moment of Reflection 2.9: Multiple Perspectives

Before you read the letter from Bigi Luetchford, you were asked to consider the impact on a learner new to the education setting having previously been educated at a different setting or perhaps at home. Let's now consider the relationship with the parents/caregivers. How is information communicated to parents? Is there direct contact between teachers and parents? How often are reports sent and what is their purpose? What is the most common inquiry from parents? How accessible are the methods of communication? Is there anything you could adapt to or change about your practice in light of the answers to these questions?

Consider These Unifying Truths

Change is inherently unsettling. Everyone experiences some level of apprehension when encountering new situations, people or environments. This unease stems from our instinct to assess the unknown for risks and challenges. Whether stepping into a new role, joining a different social setting or embarking on a learning journey, everyone seeks a sense of security and belonging.

Every individual begins their learning journey from a unique starting point, shaped by personal experiences, prior knowledge, and cognitive frameworks. It is impossible to fully gauge the depth of someone's understanding or the complexities of their background. Judging another's competence too quickly can lead to assumptions that obscure their true potential. Genuine learning thrives in environments that recognise and respect this diversity of experience.

The fear of failure is universal. No one is immune to self-doubt, and for many, the prospect of making mistakes can be paralysing. Yet, failure is not merely an obstacle – it is an essential part of growth. When failure is met with understanding rather than judgement, individuals feel empowered to take risks, experiment and refine their skills without fear of harsh consequences. No one performs at their best when they feel out of depth, disorganised or inadequately prepared. A lack of clarity, structure or resources can hinder even the most capable individuals. When people are provided with the right tools, clear expectations and a supportive environment, they are far more likely to engage fully and achieve their potential. Recognising these truths helps us cultivate environments – whether in education, the workplace or personal relationships – where people feel safe, valued and capable of growth. By fostering understanding, individuals are encouraged to step beyond their fears and into a space of meaningful progress.

Being Mindful of Disadvantages in All Its Forms

Disadvantages of any kind can distract a person from their intentions. For example, you might arrive at an education setting with the best intentions to focus and achieve alongside your peers but sometimes it feels impossible to put worries aside.

The disadvantages can be structural which can limit access to resources and opportunities. It can also be cumulative and as a learner gets older, it becomes increasingly difficult to manage. It can be nuanced and require a person-centred approach to ensure that minimal assumptions are made. Equally disadvantage must not be assumed as a result of knowing something about a learner that fits a stereotype of disadvantage, as without knowing the full picture it could be deemed offensive.

Moment of Reflection 2.10: Curiosity

Consider the following questions in relation to your setting and how they may impact learning.

What is your experience of disadvantage and how might it influence your perception of the learners in your class? This can be challenging as often we have to face up to presumptions we make and admit that we are biased.

1. What is your personal experience of disadvantage?
2. How do you feel that has shaped your worldview?
3. How might this limit your perspective on others with a different experience to your own?
4. How important is the context of an education setting and the surrounding community to address disadvantages?
5. How does your setting address disadvantages?
6. What data do you have on disadvantage in your setting?

Taking the Omniscient Perspective

Practitioners are used to reflecting upon how well a lesson went, what tasks worked well and what didn't, and reflective practice is a key element of most if not all practitioner training courses. However, as the demands of the classroom increase and analysis is focused on the young people in our classrooms as opposed to ourselves and our development, this level of reflection can be difficult to maintain. Schools can also direct what professional development is undertaken by staff with compulsory courses on whole school topics such as safeguarding and child protection. Time for training during the school year is limited and there is also that nagging feeling that any free time on an inset day should be devoted to planning or sorting the classroom out ready for the next term. These jobs are never ending.

However, taking some time to reflect is crucial in identifying more productive ways of working or pinch points during the day, which might be affecting overall morale. It is an opportunity to review what you do when you do what you do. Reflexive practice is not simply reflecting upon your own performance – it's viewing yourself as an actor within that situation and considering the part that you played in it.

Reflexive Thinking in Action

The Situation

A new learner has started an education setting, and you have been given some information about them from the SENCo or learning support department. They have informed you that this learner has a pupil passport which was written by their last education setting and advises the practitioners that this learner needs more time to think through their ideas and will need more time to respond to questions. You take this on board and during the first lesson you give the learner more time to respond, but they are unresponsive, and you persevere and give them another question which you consider easier for them to answer. Again, they do not respond. As it's their first day, you decide not to pursue their reluctance to participate and set a writing task. Once again, they complete the minimum and when encouraged to do more refuse. At this point, you decide that this is not acceptable behaviour and give them whatever sanction you use in your education setting. At the end of the day, you reflect upon this new learner and your response, and you decide that it was entirely justified because of their behaviour.

Reframing Using Systems Thinking

Take a step back and analyse yourself in that situation. You might consider:

- How you made decisions regarding the time that you gave that learner to respond.
- The question that you chose to rephrase and the way that you encouraged them.

If you had a learner with a similar need in the past, then your response may have been informed by this. You may not have had a learner with slow processing and therefore used a neurotypical benchmark in order to make your decisions. You will also have brought your own expectations to that situation and it's important to analyse these expectations as they may not align with the learner's expectations.

As you begin to use this reflexive practice, you can see that there were several opportunities to gain more information and shift perspective.

For example, in a conversation with the learner about their experience of learning and their capacity to take on verbal information, you might find out that they never respond in class because of a speech and language difficulty, and they are used to having a check-in with the practitioner before putting pen to paper.

Moment of Reflection 2.11: Multiple Perspectives

If you have learners with pupil passports or learner profiles, what do your learners understand about their needs? How would they describe what they need in order to access the learning?

This chapter has supported a personal inquiry into your own values, your worldview and experiences and how these might impact your practice. It encourages curiosity from the outset and is intended to inform the environment section of the VSM as well as system 1, the factory floor. It has raised questions about the current approach to curriculum planning and the considerations needed to develop a learner-centred practice. This understanding of yourself, your personal and professional perspectives, as well as keeping learners at the heart of all decisions, will be a continuous thread throughout the book.

Moments of Reflection

- 2.1 Curiosity
- 2.2 Multiple Perspectives
- 2.3 Interrelationships
- 2.4 Practice
- 2.5 Multiple Perspectives
- 2.6 Practice
- 2.7 Boundary Judgement
- 2.8 Interrelationships and Boundary Judgements
- 2.9 Multiple Perspectives
- 2.10 Curiosity
- 2.11 Multiple Perspectives

References

1) Department of Education. (2023). *Special educational needs in England: January 2023*. www.gov.uk/government/statistics/special-educational-needs-in-england-january-2023
2) Richmond, T. (2021). *Speed read: Think tank calls for GCSEs to be scrapped by 2025*. https://schoolsweek.co.uk/speed-read-think-tank-calls-for-gcses-to-be-scrapped-by-2025

3

SEND, the Present and the Future

Overview

As the focus moves from the wide perspective of the environment and starts to consider the more immediate surroundings, it is important to continue with a deeper analysis of SEND. Referring back to the VSM, this chapter relates to System 4 – intelligence, opportunities and threats. It seeks to **be** informed by governance and **to** inform planning and organisation on a setting and practitioner level. What emerges from this chapter are questions relating to *'known knowns'*, and opportunities to start to challenge them if they are no longer fit for purpose or they do not place the learner at the centre of the action. It evaluates historical education developments before considering the SEND framework and its current context. It finishes with a call to action and encourages reflection through the use of a Strategic Options Development Analysis (SODA) map. This in-depth approach highlights key goals to focus on and measures for effectiveness over the coming months. It starts big and homes in on manageable targets whilst not losing sight of the bigger picture. The results of this analysis can then be used to inform system 4 in regard to the intelligence gathered through this exercise and the subsequent opportunities it presents to inform **plannin**g (system 3), **communication** (system 2) and **production** (system 1).

Slowly, a system is emerging . . . So far, the overall system has been introduced, followed by a consideration of the practitioner's role and the learners in the classroom.

DOI: 10.4324/9781003400639-4

This chapter considers how SEND is defined and how our understanding of SEND has been shaped in education. There is a need for labels in order to identify the support required and assign resource. Whilst identifying SEND means differentiating learners from the 'mainstream', it is a necessary facet of the current education system. If perhaps the system was more accommodating to individual difference, the need for specific labels might decrease. However, homogeneity is also not the answer to making a classroom more equitable. There is a synergy between a systems approach and the transdiagnosis research which is explored later in this chapter. A systems approach sees difficulties not as isolated problems but as patterns that emerge and transdiagnostic research also resists siloed categories, focusing instead on processes that cut across diagnoses. Later in the chapter the co-occurrence of specific learning difficulties in relation to key learning skills is explored and it is evident that there are patterns in skills which would benefit from a more holistic rather than linear approach.

Starting new topics: a system routine with targeted supports

A learner with anxiety and dyslexia starts a new topic. Novelty and uncertainty reduce working-memory capacity and narrow attention. Dyslexia slows decoding, increases errors, and makes written expression effortful. If anxiety stays undisclosed, a practitioner may notice dyslexia and offer reading and writing support, while missing scaffolds for the novelty and uncertainty which anxiety will exacerbate. This mismatch will build frustration for both the practitioner and learner. A system response suggested below would mitigate for the additional demands of a new topic and then layer targeted support where needed.

Recommendations for new topic introductions

1. Preview the learning map. Give a one page overview, key terms, success criteria.
2. Surface previous knowledge. Deliver a mini quiz, group or pair discussions and adjust approach according to knowledge in the room.
3. Chunk the first lesson. Short blocks of study and regular retrieval checks.
4. Offer dual channels. Spoken explanation plus visual guides. Short video clips and annotated notes.

5. Build low stakes practice. Try it tasks with immediate feedback.
6. Provide options for output. Oral response, writing frames or a structured template. Remove the scaffolds as expertise grows.
7. Set predictable timings. Lesson outline on the board with time expectations.
8. Close with a final check. One question or confidence rating to guide the next step.

Targeted layer for disclosed literacy difficulties:

- Accessible text for all levels in the classroom
- Guided notes with word banks or sentence stems
- Alternative options to record information to handwriting

Targeted layer for anxiety:

- Pre-lesson preview or script of what to expect in this lesson
- Option to sit near a trusted peer and away from distractions as much as possible
- Scheduled check in before independent work

SEND remains underfunded (BBC, 2025), and there is a lack of specialist training for all school staff in this area. Whilst pedagogy is covered in-depth on teacher training courses, they often lack the depth needed to address the complexities of SEND. Initial teacher training can include SEND professionals' contributions; these are likely to be standalone sessions. SEND may be covered through CPD in education settings; it often remains needs-led or part of elective study rather than comprehensive. For any initiative to be successful, it requires commitment and support from the senior leadership team and long-term planning. Especially in relation to understanding individual needs related to learning difficulties. However, due to the complex nature of SEND and the interrelated factors, a commitment to addressing SEND in a school can be difficult to identify and implement in spite of an education setting's commitment or will to change.

Moment of Reflection 3.1: Curiosity

Part 1. What is it about meeting the needs of those with learning differences that is so challenging? Approach this with an honest and open mind and list everything you can think of.

Moment of Reflection 3.2: Interrelationships

Part 2. Now reflect upon these challenges from a VSM system 4 perspective – this is the system which deals with intelligence, opportunities and threats. Consider what challenges are as a result of the system rather than the individual and how intelligence from governance or the environment informs the strategies to address these challenges. For example, what is the provision for managing transition for learners with anxiety or autism? Is this evidence-based, what the education setting has always done or informed by the learners themselves?

You might have found the above exercise difficult as there are few definitive answers relating to either the challenges the learner faces in the classroom or the ability to identify the root cause. Often, difficulties do not happen in a linear fashion and can be unpredictable making planning even more challenging. Supporting those with additional needs could be considered a 'wicked problem*'. There are so many moving parts when you think about SEND it quickly becomes a subject which unravels, twists and tangles with every new question or initiative. Whilst education settings are working hard to address recognised learning difficulties, other complexities emerge which don't fit recognised patterns and are perhaps a result of environmental factors such as COVID or digital media.

The following insight is from Dave Barrett, an experienced specialist teacher and leader in education who supports schools in developing their practice to support those who are finding learning a challenge. As a dyslexia assessor, Dave spends every day working closely with people who find learning hard and through the assessment process often provides them with some answers to their struggles. Dave combines his knowledge of specific learning difficulties with his experience in the classroom, and below are his top tips for an inclusive classroom.

Moment of Reflection 3.3: Practice

As you read Dave's letter, consider your own practice in relation to his suggestions and what is in your control to change and what is not. Is there flexibility in your setting to trial new approaches or is there an expectation from the setting that teaching is delivered in a specific manner? If this is the case, how does that align with your values?

Dear practitioner,

It is a pleasure to be able to write to you about the benefits and importance of providing an inclusive classroom and learning opportunities for all learners, regardless of any identified need. It is my belief that all learners would have strengths and weaknesses in their cognitive profile, and most would benefit from a pre-planned inclusive classroom and a more accessible curriculum.

Inclusive practice is known by many terms: quality first teaching, inclusive classrooms and dyslexia-friendly learning. Essentially the practice is the same, regardless of which term is used. The DfE measures inclusion as a school which can 'remove barriers to learning and provide an education which is appropriate to the learners' needs'. There are many simple, effective steps and 'quick wins' that can be implemented to create a positive and welcoming environment for all learners.

Understanding and supporting the impact that a learner's memory ability can have on their learning is a key component of an inclusive classroom.

Memory challenges can affect many learners, irrespective of their intelligence, and implementing support strategies will benefit large cohorts in many classrooms. Rather than just supporting those with identified memory challenges, inclusive classrooms take the whole class approach. This ensures that the learner does not feel singled out for their needs but also helps support those without an identified need.

Simplifying language, reducing the amount of verbal information provided and giving learners both verbal and visual instructions all help support their understanding and recall of tasks. Instructions can be broken down into manageable stages on a visual planning sheet, often next to the teacher's board in class, and be reused for each task set. This helps support their ability to refer to and work through a task independently and scaffolds their learning into manageable chunks.

Writing frames are further examples of scaffolded learning. Breaking down tasks or instructions into smaller sections to complete in turn often results in more output than an extended task; the importance of smaller steps for some learners cannot be underestimated.

Overlearning and embedding regular recall of previously learnt topics is also crucial.

Research shows that immediately after a lesson, the ability to recall its content drops significantly, with people often only being able to recall 30% of the content after 24 hours. Regular recaps on key content and overlearning will help support retention and do not have to detract from the next lesson's content. Often a quick peer-to-peer discussion at the start of the lesson about the previous topic can provide a good level of recall.

Using visuals as a resource to assist within the classroom can help support learners to successfully retain information.

Many practitioners embed the use of visuals for those with speech and language or communication and interaction needs, but they are also extremely effective for whole class learning and support.

Visuals can provide routine and structure through visual timetables which are effective for many learners. They can also be used for reinforcing concepts (especially new or technical vocabulary), supporting verbal requests, offering choices and prompting communication. For many learners, the use of visuals, alongside written information, can help speed up their understanding and ease the recall of newly learnt information.

The layout and environment of a classroom is also an important factor to consider.

From an organisational perspective, having resources easily available, effective working wall displays, multisensory learning opportunities and visuals to support new vocabulary all helps support the progress and flow of a lesson. It is also important to consider the physical environment of a classroom. The temperature, ventilation and lighting in the classroom are all conducive to a positive learning environment. Many learners will display challenges with their sensory behaviours, and many will be affected by visual distortions and discomfort when working in bright environments. Using natural lighting where possible, pastel shaded backgrounds on electronic screens, coloured overlays and paper can all make a significant difference in making the classroom and the learning content much clearer and more comfortable to focus on and therefore easier to understand and retain.

A further key component of an inclusive classroom is the ability to allow learners to access and present their learning differently. The 2019 Ofsted inspection framework valued the importance of this approach where they state that they want to see learners provided with 'multiple means of representation'. Allowing learners to create mind maps, dictate answers, use a reader, colour code, create posters etc. are all examples of ways that a lesson's objective can be more easily achieved for many. This approach can take time to embed and feel confident with, and I'd suggest trialling some approaches initially. Many schools have implemented a 'no pens day' to see what creative opportunities can be provided to their learners.

With the advancing field of assistive technology, providing an inclusive classroom and learning opportunities is no longer adding to the workload of an already difficult role. It can often be seen as the opposite, with technology being able to be used to easily provide inclusive measures which support both the learner and the practitioner. Speech to text, mind mapping, text to speech and colour filter software are all examples which may benefit learners. There are also many applications, often free to schools, which allow the practitioner to create electronic files as evidence in addition to books. This allows the class team to be able to easily record, photograph or provide other creative opportunities to capture their learning and therefore demonstrate their progress easily.

The development of an inclusive classroom can lead to a more positive and calmer learning environment.

It can also often result in a reduction in the SEND register as many of the learners' needs are being adequately met. Such approaches have a positive impact on individual learners' learning and self-esteem and can also allow the whole class to demonstrate progress in a faster and easier way.

David Barrett

Specialist practitioner and SEND consultant

Systems Thinking and the UK Education System

Whilst this section relates to the changes in the UK education system, international readers might like to reflect on the development of their own education systems and draw comparisons with the UK model as outlined below.

Let's consider the education system and the influences on it starting with the government. Changes in government often mean changes to national services such as health and education. This is inevitable, but can result in a period of uncertainty whilst new ways of working are becoming embedded in setting.

The introduction of academies over the last 20 years has been a government-led initiative to encourage additional funding from the private sector into education settings and a way of providing increased flexibility for those running successful settings as well as a way to support failing education settings by placing them under the wing of a successful academy, bringing with it the expertise and resources of that organisation. Academies are not reliant on the local authority (LA) and can therefore develop their own resources related to training and supporting learning differences. They are free to employ their own specialists and commission the services of experts to inform teaching and learning.

The growth of academies has reduced transparency in governance and increased inconsistency within and between trusts. This raises the risk of fragmentations and selection effects that local authority oversight once moderated. SEND demand is rising in England, with the number of learners identified with SEND increasing year on year since 2016 (DfE, 2024, 2025; POST, 2025). The capacity for professional services, outside the education setting, has not kept pace. Delays and uneven access follow. These pressures slow school improvement and continue to widen the gap in performance from those with additional needs.

In systems terms, academisation changes information flows and decision rights. Rising SEND need is an inflow. Specialist staffing is a constrained stock. Bottlenecks and delays create reinforcing loops of inequity. Share data, pooled commissioning of specialist services and clear local protocols form balancing loops that restore coordination. This would require greater collaboration between local settings and some academies are national which would make this more challenging.

Moment of Reflection 3.4: Multiple Perspectives

As you reflect on the timeline below, consider your thoughts and feelings around the changes and whether you discussed any of them with your colleagues, relations or friends at the time.

Do some of the changes have a different impact depending on the role you are playing in the system? For example:

- A parent/carer
- A learner
- A member of support staff
- A teacher
- A leader

Which changes have had a lasting impact?

Timeline of Changes in the English Education System (2004–2024)

2004–2012: Introduction of Academies

2004: The Academies Programme expands, allowing struggling education settings to convert into semi-independent academies with more freedom from LAs and control over their budgets and curricula.

2006: The Education and Inspections Act reinforces the academies' expansion, encouraging more education settings to convert to academy status.

2010: The Academies Act is passed, leading to a significant increase in the number of academies, including outstanding education settings, which could now convert to academy status.

2012: Michael Gove, then Secretary of State for Education, announces a review of the National Curriculum, emphasising a more knowledge-based curriculum with a focus on traditional subjects.

2012: Phasing out of modular GCSEs begins, replaced by a system where all exams are taken at the end of the course.

2013–2017: Introduction of New GCSEs and A-Levels

2013: Introduction of the Pupil Premium, providing additional funding to education settings for disadvantaged pupils.

2014: New, tougher GCSEs begin to be introduced, with a focus on end-of-course exams and reduced coursework. These changes are phased in over several years.

2015: The Conservative government under David Cameron commits to further expanding academies, aiming for all education settings to become academies or free schools by 2022.

2016: Introduction of Progress 8 as the main accountability measure for secondary education settings, which assesses learners' progress across eight subjects.

2017: The traditional A*–G grading system for GCSEs is replaced by a numerical 9–1 scale, with 9 being the highest grade. This change is phased in, with different subjects adopting the new grading system in different years.

2018–2020: Mental Health and Well-Being Focus

2019: The new Ofsted framework places greater emphasis on the quality of education, behaviour, and attitudes, as well as personal development, moving away from a narrow focus on exam results.

2020: Education setting closures due to the COVID-19 pandemic lead to a rapid shift to online learning. The disruption caused the cancellation of GCSEs and A-levels, with grades awarded based on practitioner assessments and a controversial algorithm.

2020: The government launches a National Tutoring Programme to help pupils catch up on lost learning due to the pandemic.

2021: Post-COVID-19 Adjustments

2021: Continued adjustments to exams and assessments due to ongoing disruptions from COVID-19, including further reliance on practitioner assessments and modified exams.

2021: The Skills for Jobs White Paper is published, emphasising the need for technical education and lifelong learning, with a focus on further education colleges and apprenticeships.

2022–2024: Current Trends and Developments

2022: The government continues to push for a more skills-based education system, with increasing emphasis on vocational qualifications and T Levels as alternatives to A-levels.

2023: Ofsted begins to pilot new inspection frameworks that focus more on curriculum depth and breadth, with less emphasis on data and more on the holistic educational experience of learners.

2024: Ongoing debates and potential reforms around the role of exams in the education system, with discussions about balancing academic and vocational pathways and the future of GCSEs.

The changes highlighted for the purpose of this book are by no means the most important or the only ones due consideration but have been selected for their relation to systems thinking and special educational needs. Getting the right support in place for a learner with persistent and lifelong learning difficulties has always been hard for both education settings and parents. A statement of special educational needs was replaced by the **Education, Health and Care Plan** in 2014 in an attempt to ensure that a learner's education and health needs were considered and planned for using the same document rather than having multiple approaches. These plans are intended for use until the learner reaches 25 years of age and uses the four areas of need from the SEND Code of Practice which are explored later in this chapter.

Moment of Reflection 3.5: Practice

How many of the learners you work with have an Education, Health and Care Plan (EHCP)? How do you implement the recommendations from the EHCP and monitor their impact? How many of the learners you work with would benefit from an EHCP? Do you think there could be a better system for identifying and meeting the needs of learners with learning difficulties?

Causal Loop of Disadvantage and the Impact on Learning

The advantage of this visual tool is that it can highlight what is known but also what is underestimated in terms of negative feedback. It might be known that disadvantage affects learning but how and where that impact is felt the most can be difficult to discern.

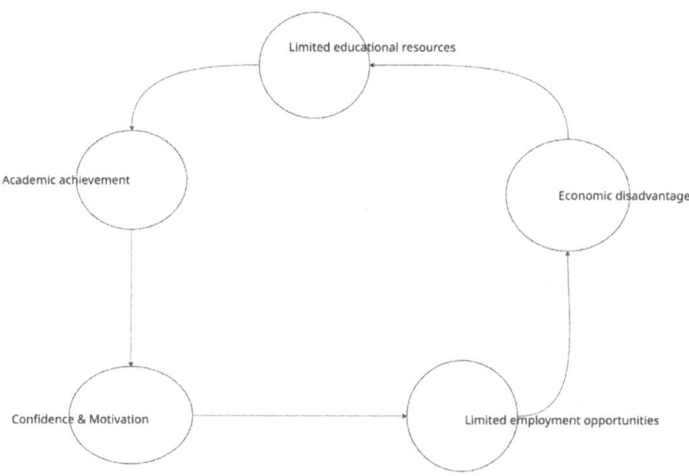

Figure 3.1 A causal loop of disadvantage

Moment of Reflection 3.6: Interrelationships

The causal loop diagram in Figure 3.1 shows how any disadvantage can impact progress in education. It can create a cycle which is difficult to break. Each arrow shows the negative direction of the relationship. Evaluate the impact intervention at each point of the causal loop might have and where the knock-on effect might be? Consider whether this effect is positive or negative. Don't be constrained by thinking only about your role or your education setting when considering your options. This is a theoretical exercise.

This is a website to add causes to a causal loop and animate them: https://ncase.me/loopy. It helps to see the positive and negative relationships between causes. Use it to explore disadvantages and the impact on specific aspects of learning. Experiment with adding and subtracting causal factors and reflect on your findings.

For a reminder about the steps to creating a causal loop diagram refer back to Chapter 1.

Systemic Leadership and Increased Autonomy

Ainscow (2019) in *Changing Education Systems: A Research-Based Approach* highlights how fundamental power is to systemic reform. Multi-academy trusts (MATs) have the opportunity to create networks of schools and learn from each other, making the most use of limited budgets and sharing expertise across several schools rather than there being pockets of brilliant teaching that remain exclusive to one school. Ainscow points out that countries across the world are looking to improve their national education system and many of these are looking at increasing autonomy. The theory behind increasing autonomy in schools is that this will enable them to make better decisions to promote the learning of their learners; there will be less time to wait for agreements over classroom, practice and finance or regulations and more opportunity to address the needs of their cohort of learners. However, increased autonomy brings with it high levels of competition and this may further disadvantage learners from low income or minority families.

There are several important implications regarding funding for education settings which will determine their actions and where their focus may lie. Ofsted and the impact of an unfavourable inspection can damage an education setting and its staff for years. Whilst education settings may not be inspected every year, there is always that cloud hanging over education settings of inspection. Some education setting places are hotly contested due to highly populated areas or a lack of other perceived good education settings. Then there are exam results and the

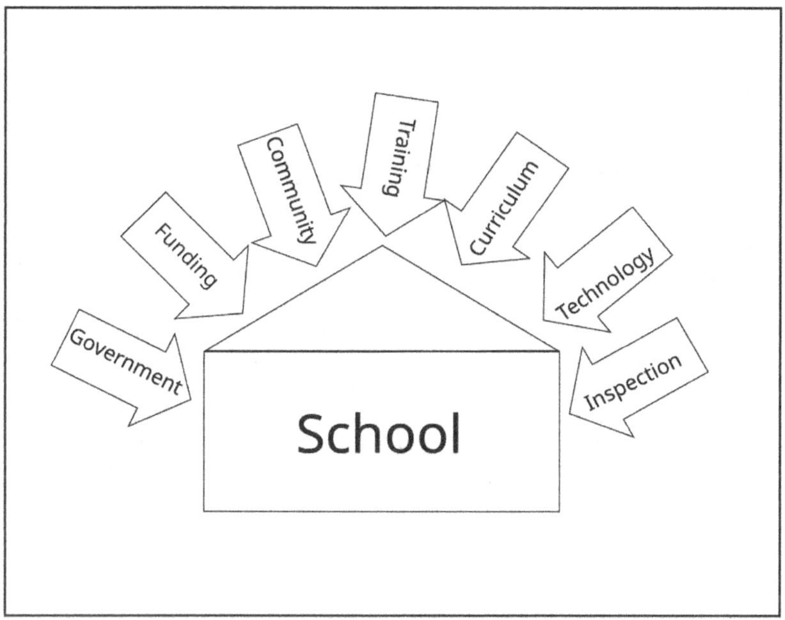

Figure 3.2 The pressures on education settings

higher education paths that learners take or the community and sporting links an education setting may have.

Ofsted's Guidance for SEND (2022)

Ofsted guidance for special educational needs and disabilities (SEND) sets out how Ofsted inspectors will assess the quality of provision for learners and young people with SEND. The guidance covers all aspects of SEND provision, from identification and assessment to support and outcomes.

Some of the key areas that inspectors will focus on include:

- The accuracy and timeliness of identification and assessment: Inspectors will check that learners and young people with SEND are identified accurately and that their needs are assessed in a timely way.
- The quality of support: Inspectors will look at the quality of support that learners and young people with SEND receive, including the quality of

teaching, the availability of specialist provision, and the effectiveness of parental involvement.
- The outcomes for learners and young people: Inspectors will assess the progress that learners and young people with SEND make, and whether they are achieving the same outcomes as their peers without SEND.

Moment of Reflection 3.7: Boundary Judgements

As you are likely becoming a systems thinker by now, reflect for a moment on the language used in the Ofsted guidance.

Does it feel empowering for the learner?

Is it promoting a whole education setting approach or discrete provision?

Is it enough?

The SEND Code of Practice Surpasses Its Tenth Birthday: Is It Time for a Proper Update?

The SEND Code of Practice (Department of Education & Department of Health and Social Care, 2014) is a document which covers a huge breadth of learning differences as well as provisions and was designed to help identify and streamline support for learners who were on SEND registers. It reinforced the important recommendation that **every teacher is a teacher of SEND** and gave SENCos more power to ensure that the needs of learners with SENCo were being met by the class practitioner and not through outside-of-the-classroom interventions. Preceding these changes there was some concern that learners were on the SEND register without due cause and too many learners had been incorrectly identified for SEND when it was a pastoral need. SENCos provided some pushback before providing support in the **graduated approach** and encouraged practitioners to try quality first teaching approaches before requesting support.

The graduated approach is a cycle of **assess, plan, do** and **review** and gives the SENCo a structure with which to explain to class practitioners how referrals to explore a learner's needs would be dealt with and the outcomes.

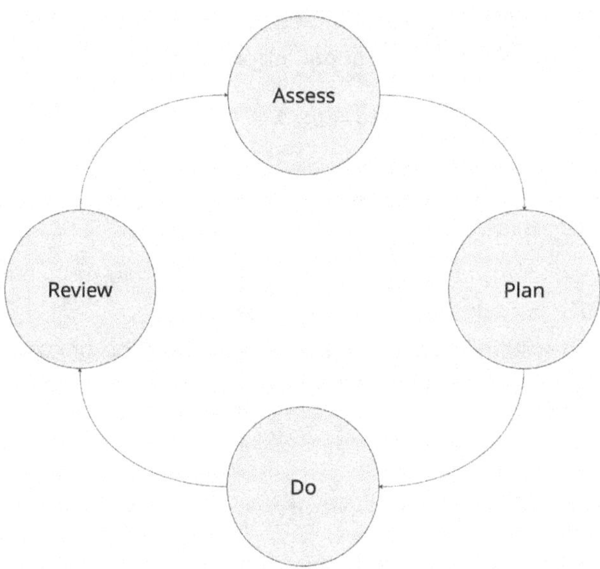

Figure 3.3 Graduated approach

Table 3.1 The advantages and disadvantages of the graduated approach

Advantages of the Graduated Approach	*Considerations of the Graduated Approach*
Clear cycle of assessment and support to follow	No time frames
Opportunity to build an evidence base to support any further requests for resources	Potential to get stuck in the cycle
Time to reflect on the efficacy of an approach is factored in	May be a question of ownership and therefore a lack of progress as a result of the uncertainty

In 2022, there was a SEND review (Department of Education & Department of Health and Social Care, 2022) which highlighted:

- the inconsistencies in the EHCP process
- the quality of the plans across the UK
- the long wait for assessments including speech and language, autism, ADHD and specific learning difficulties such as dyslexia and dyscalculia
- the continued poor outcomes for those learners with SEND.

It suggested a new SEND Code of Practice, which is currently still in development that would recommend, among other things:

- national standard for SEND provision
- standardised EHCP templates
- improved accountability frameworks for MATS, LAs and health bodies
- early intervention reducing the reliance on EHCPs
- greater support for families early on in education to reduce the potential for an EHCP later in the learner's education
- a simplified system which will reduce the likelihood of cases going to tribunal, reducing the stress for families and cost to the state.

Moment of Reflection 3.8: Curiosity

Consider what you think would need to change in order for the changes above to work? On a scale of 1 being impossible to 5 being simple, how easy would it be to align structures, behaviours and outcomes?

As you consider your answers to the above, consider system 4, what opportunities would such changes bring and how could they inform your planning and organisation (system 3), what needs to be communicated from system 5 in order to reduce potential threats?

Is the Term SEND Outdated and Should That Also Be Updated?

Both special educational needs and disability can, for some parents/carers, cause concern and make them reluctant to seek support for their child or young person for fear of either labelling them or limiting their opportunities. There is also the stigma that the child or young person may experience for being othered and separated from their peers.

Most education settings work hard at integrating learners with SEND but often have a SEND unit or place where those with additional needs can seek support if needed. This can provide a haven but also an escape route from doing hard things. Learning is hard, acquiring knowledge is hard, and maintaining the focus and processing capacity required is sometimes impossible for some learners. BUT . . . learners are naturally curious and want to understand and make sense of the world around them.

Identifying Need Using the Four Areas of Need from the SEND Code of Practice

If the first step to supporting SEND in the classroom according to the SEND Code of Practice is a graduated approach for the whole cohort, the second step is to identify individual needs.

The SEND Code of Practice identified four areas of need, and it is expected that the majority of learning difficulties fall within one of these areas. It's important to highlight that whilst the four areas are separate, it is more common for learners and young people to have a combination of difficulties than one particular single difficulty.

The four areas are cognition and learning, physical and sensory needs, communication and interaction and social, emotional and mental health. They can provide practitioners with guidelines to understanding the different areas of need, and also by combining them with the graduated approach, it provides an easily understandable, and more importantly transferable, language with which education settings and educational professionals can discuss learners with additional support needs.

Moment of Reflection 3.9: Practice

As you read the descriptions of the four areas, you are likely to already be familiar with these – is there an area which you have most experience with? Does this influence your practice? Is there an area which you know least about? What support is there in your setting to develop your knowledge?

Cognition and Learning

The **SEND Code of Practice (Department of Education & Department of Health and Social Care, 2014)** defines cognition and learning as 'the ways in which learners think, understand and learn'. It includes a wide range of needs, from specific learning difficulties (such as dyslexia) to more general learning difficulties.

Learners with cognition and learning needs may experience difficulties in a number of areas, including:

- Reading: They may find it difficult to decode words, understand what they have read, or both.
- Writing: They may have difficulty forming letters, spelling words correctly, or expressing their ideas in writing.
- Mathematics: They may have difficulty understanding number concepts, performing calculations, or solving problems.
- Social and emotional development: They may have difficulty understanding social cues, making friends, or managing their emotions.

The SEND Code of Practice emphasises the importance of early identification and intervention for learners with cognition and learning needs.

Physical and Sensory Needs

The SEND Code of Practice defines physical and sensory needs as follows:

Physical needs are those that affect a learner's ability to move around, use their body or access the environment. They can be caused by a wide range of conditions, including physical disabilities, long-term health conditions and injuries.

Sensory needs are those that affect a learner's ability to see, hear, smell, taste or touch. They can be caused by a wide range of conditions, including hearing impairment, visual impairment, multisensory impairment and autism.

Learners with physical and sensory needs may require additional support and/or equipment to access the curriculum and participate in education setting activities. This support can be provided by a range of professionals, including practitioners, teaching assistants, therapists and support staff.

Communication and Interaction

Learners with speech, language and communication needs have difficulty in communicating with others. This may be because they have difficulty saying what they want to, understanding what is being said to them, or they do not understand or use social rules of communication.

It can be difficult with receptive language; the language heard and subsequently understood in order to respond. Or it can be an expressive language; the language used to get a message across.

Learners with communication and interaction needs may need support with understanding tasks and instructions as well as expressing themselves. They might also need support interpreting the world around them and that will include social situations.

Social, Emotional and Mental Health

Learners may experience a wide range of social and emotional difficulties which manifest in many ways. These may include becoming withdrawn or isolated, as well as displaying challenging or disruptive behaviour. These behaviours may reflect underlying mental health difficulties such as anxiety or depression, self-harm or physical symptoms that are medically unexplained.

The world is a very different place to what it was over ten years ago, and there is a need for an updated approach to education and a review of SEND practices in education settings. The cases of SEND are rising in both primary and secondary schools with the increase in EHCPs over the last five years. This is the tip of the iceberg however, with the level of need from those with undiagnosed difficulties being unknown. Added to this are the lack of spaces in special schools as well as the increase in homeschooled learners, some of whom are may flourish through homeschooling but there are many who are marginalised and missing out on an education.

Moment of Reflection 3.10: Interrelationships

Consider your current environment and if these four categories fit the learners you see in education settings. Have they remained as four separate areas?

Is there one which dominates over another?

It is often the case that in the early years it is communication and interaction needs which are most prevalent. In primary schools, it is cognition and learning, and in secondary schools it is social, emotional and mental health needs. There is an expectation that when a learner reaches secondary school they have the basic foundations of learning; primary education is about developing skills and secondary school is about applying them. In recent years, there has been an increase in learners not presenting as being ready for their new phase in education, with more learners starting reception in nappies and unable to hold cutlery, to Key Stage 1 starters having emerging reading and writing skills rather than achieving some mastery of phonics and letter shapes. Learners start secondary schools without the foundation skills of literacy and numeracy necessary to engage in subjects at a deeper level.

The Foundation Skill of Reading

Without being able to read fluently, it is difficult to comprehend and respond to text. Reading fluency can impact sentences as well as full passages of text. The lack of automaticity slows the process of reading down, taking more processing capacity, and can lead to feelings of stress and tiredness due to the extra effort. Education remains heavily reliant on written information.

A helpful image of the strands required in building reading skills is **Scarborough's (2001) reading rope**. Whilst Hollis Scarborough never set out with the intention to shape literacy provision with this analysis of reading skills, it persists as a useful example which serves as a reminder of the different strands/skills required to be a fluent reader. It also highlights the need to continue to combine both strands instead of assuming that mastery over some of the strands is universal by a certain age.

There is a growing need in secondary education settings to continue building word knowledge rather than assume this skill has been accomplished at an earlier stage in a learner's education. This fixed mindset of what is expected of learners due to historical assumptions about literacy

Figure 3.4 Circles and rectangle doors

skills acquisition and the consequential rigidity of a system to support individual differences causes friction for all involved. It is the round peg in a square hole scenario.

This shift in skills (I am reluctant to label it as a decline as this may mask improvements made in skills elsewhere and be overly negative) cannot be pinpointed to a single cause, nor should it be, as it is part of a complex and messy situation.

Educational needs appear to be changing. This was perhaps highlighted by COVID as during the lockdowns parents gained increased insight into how their learners learn. This led to a spike in referrals for learning difficulties.

When a difficulty either with behaviour or learning is identified, parents often face a wait. This wait can be weeks, months or even years. Their learner may leave one education setting for another or even leave an education setting entirely before they are assessed. As mentioned before, our system is built and somewhat reliant on these labels and it is therefore almost essential that parents find an answer to their child's challenges with literacy or behaviour before intervention is provided.

The SEND Code of Practice (2014) stated that **quality first teaching** should be the first approach to meeting the needs of a learner who is struggling. A SENCo may often recommend a handful of strategies and encourage the practitioner or teaching assistant to implement this for a few weeks before measuring the impact. In addition to the long wait to receive a diagnosis, there is also the challenge of meeting the needs of some learners who might have a number of learning and behavioural difficulties and their experience in education is one of challenge and difficulty. This might be experienced by them but also by their practitioner and their classmates. The disruption caused by an unhappy and disengaged learner can be the dominating factor in a teacher's planning, delivery and management of their classroom. Whilst the wait for a diagnosis is related to funding, since COVID there has been an increased dissatisfaction with the education system and potentially an impression that homeschooling is easier than it looks. In the summer term of 2023, the Department for Education estimated that approximately 97,000 learners were home educated (Adams, 2024), an increase of 11,000 from the previous term. There are now several online schools and homeschool hubs, so parents who live in the right areas can access a varied and rich curriculum for their learners without having to open a textbook themselves. This is very much a lottery and likely to be far easier for parents living near big cities than for those in rural areas.

Alongside a change in learning needs identified in education settings, how learning difficulties are defined has also changed over the last ten years. Asperger's syndrome is no longer referred to as a separate condition, but comes under the umbrella of autism. It was often used to describe people at the milder end of the autistic spectrum, but was phased out from 2013 due to an update of the DSM-5 (APA, 2013) which reclassified it under the broader category of autism spectrum disorder.

Around the same time, the term attention deficit disorder was also recategorised under the umbrella term of attention deficit hyperactivity disorder (ADHD), but with added categories that covered inattentive, hyperactivity-impulsive presentation, or combined. ADD was phased out in 1987 but the current definitions have been in place since 2013.

Moment of Reflection 3.11: Curiosity

Reflect for a moment on the benefit of a learning difficulty being described as a spectrum.

What does this elimination of a specific cut-off do?

Does this feel a fairer approach or could we do even better?

It is evident that the definition of a learning difficulty is somewhat subjective and can evolve with the needs of the people being assessed. But specific learning difficulties remain separate definitions for which each requires a diagnosis. For example, if a person is considered to have all three it might require three separate assessments. Each will come with their own recommendations and suggested ways of working, some of which, might, in fact, be in competition with each other.

Understanding Neurodiversity and Neurodivergence

In recent years the landscape of learning and cognitive difference has shifted. Alongside rising diagnoses of difficulties such as ADHD, autism and dyslexia and with referral waiting lists still frustratingly long, there has been a growing call for a move towards a social model of difficulties. This cultural movement grounded in inclusion and strength-based practice has brought the term **neurodiversity** into wider use.

Neurodiversity is societal and emphasises neurological differences such as autism, ADHD and dyslexia as well as others that are not inherently pathological but part of the diversity of the human population. This is similar to biodiversity or cultural diversity. This has been further developed to incorporate and recognise the co-occurrence of mental health difficulties and their impact on a person's ability to process information. The advantage of such a term is that it does not pigeonhole a person or create an artificial hierarchy of needs but recognises the ebb and flow of a person's learning ability and how it can manifest differently due to the environment or task.

Neurodiversity is a framework, not a diagnosis. It challenges the deficit-based models of learning and mental health and instead encourages environments to adapt rather than expecting the individual to conform. What may appear as a difficulty in one environment might be a strength in another. Individuals whose brains function in ways that **diverge** from what is typically expected are described as **neurodivergent**. Neurodivergent refers to an individual. The term neurodivergence can include people with diagnoses and those who experience cognitive differences but do not identify with or do not yet have a diagnostic label.

Using the language of neurodiversity can be a non-threatening way to open conversation with learners, especially those unsure or uncomfortable with formal labels. This chapter encourages you to hold both perspectives regarding diagnoses and neurodiversity. Practitioners often walk a line between empowering learners through choice and identity and advocating effectively within systems that still rely on diagnostic labels for support funding and policy decisions.

Furthermore, it encourages a positive, affirmative approach rather than a focus on the deficits a person has. The disadvantage of such a label is that it is general as opposed to specific and therefore open to interpretation. This can lead to a lack of action or support being implemented based on one person's understanding of the term, which might be heavily influenced by a certain approach for example. An understanding of ADHD will result in strategies that focus on time management, structures and management, whereas a dyslexic approach will focus on the accessibility of the information shared by the organisation.

Table 3.2 The advantages and disadvantages of neurodiversity and specific learning difficulty (SpLD) labels

Advantages of a Neurodiverse Approach	*Disadvantages*	*Advantages of a SpLD Label*	*Disadvantages*
Chosen by person	Ambiguity	Familiarity	Often assigned TO a person
More inclusive of all needs	Novel	Established routes to support	Could mean one SpLD could become the dominant approach
Empowering	May result in a delay to support due to ambiguity	Widely understood	

Moment of Reflection 3.12: Interrelationships

Consider the pros and cons to labels and the more overarching term of neurodiversity. What do your learners understand by known learning difficulties such as autism, ADHD and dyslexia and are they familiar with neurodiversity?

Transdiagnostic: An Emerging Perspective

Recent research has increasingly challenged the traditional notion that mental health and neurodevelopment conditions are entirely discrete categories. The transdiagnostic approach suggests that many of these conditions share common underlying processes, meaning that symptoms and risk factors often cut across the boundaries of established diagnostic labels. This perspective has significant implications not only for clinical practice but also for educational interventions, where a focus on shared cognitive and emotional difficulties may offer more effective support for learners.

Shared Underlying Mechanisms

Several studies have highlighted that conditions such as dyslexia, ADHD, and anxiety may not be as categorically distinct as once thought. For example, research by Caspi et al. (2014) introduced the idea of a general psychopathology factor, often termed the 'p factor', which suggests that a common set of vulnerabilities underlies a range of difficulties. Similarly, neuro-imaging studies (e.g., Snyder et al., 2015) have demonstrated overlapping patterns of brain network dysfunction across different diagnostic groups, reinforcing the argument for a transdiagnostic framework.

For example, a learner who is struggling with anxiety, has trouble focusing in class and completing assignments, may be experiencing periods of low mood and can be prone to irrational or impulsive behaviour could be diagnosed with several separate conditions, such as ADHD, dyslexia, anxiety and depression. This could take months, maybe years of assessment, whilst the learner continues to struggle and potentially experiences further difficulties, and is likely to become, if they are not already, a poor attender. If all the factors that this learner was experiencing were looked at systematically – their home life, biological factors and learning ability (cognitive assessment), trauma and disadvantage – the plan developed would reduce the potential for misunderstanding caused by only focusing on one element of the bigger picture.

Moment of Reflection 3.13: Interrelationships

Consider this approach to mental health and neurodiversity and reflect upon the learners you might have in your setting who might have more than one diagnosis, considering their needs as a whole rather than related to their diagnoses. What, if anything, emerges from this reflection? Are there common denominators and if there are, what can you do to address these?

Implications for Educational Practice

In the educational context, a transdiagnostic approach encourages practitioners to look beyond rigid diagnostic labels and instead focus on the specific cognitive, behavioural and emotional processes that affect learning. Apperly et al (2024) report that variation in neurodiversity traits is best explained by one general factor of neurodiversity plus four condition-specific factors. This supports a transdiagnostic view of overlapping traits across diagnoses. It could be suggested that by targeting these overlapping difficulties, interventions can be more readily adapted to individual learners, regardless of their formal diagnosis.

Future Directions and Considerations

Transdiagnostic findings indicate possible benefits of integrated, systems-aware assessment and support but stronger education-sector evidence is needed before policy changes. Further research is required in this approach in education before any shift in policy is made. Rather than relying on diagnostic labels alone, practitioners and clinicians might use continuous trait-based assessment to identify shared needs and track progress over time. This approach aligns with Universal Design for Learning principles (UDL; CAST, 2024) which promote flexible environments that accommodate learner variability through multiple means of engagement, representation, and action and expression.

The key principles of UDL are as follows:

1. Multiple means of engagement (the why of learning):
    - Clarity of purpose: Harness curiosity, increase motivation and engagement.
    - Providing several examples: Multiple opportunities for learners to identify with the material, linking content to their personal experiences and interests. Using collaborative projects and personal goal settings.
2. Multiple means of representation (the what of learning):
    - Offer various ways to acquire and understand content. Be mindful of the ways you deliver content. Consider presenting the information in multiple ways such as visuals, accessible digital tools, hands-on activities, discussion groups.
3. Multiple means of action and expression (the how of learning):
    - Give the learners diverse ways to demonstrate their learning. This could include presentations, writing, multimedia projects or performance-based assessments.

The advantages of adopting a universal design for learning approach is that it encourages curiosity from the outset about a learner's ability rather than relying on historic assumptions about acquired skills. It supports inclusion from the outset with options for study incorporated in the planning from inception. It increases engagement due to a high level of learner autonomy and reduces the need for additional interventions and othering as all individual needs are part of the design.

Moreover, adopting a transdiagnostic framework can help bridge the gap between research and practice. As national directives and inspection frameworks in the UK increasingly emphasise personalised support and inclusivity in education, the evidence supporting **transdiagnostic** approaches offers a timely rationale for systemic change.

Using Systems Thinking to Explore a Setting and Identify Its Challenges and Ways to Meet Them

This book would not be useful if all it did was point out the challenges of the classroom without attempting to meet them. Therefore, the following approach will apply cognitive mapping to a classroom situation. This model of system thinking uses interrelationships and multiple perspectives to explore a situation broadly before looking for patterns to narrow it down to a few strategic tasks. The advantage of this is that the other options remain in the bigger picture and can be revisited at a later date.

Below is an example of **Strategic Options Development and Analysis (SODA)** of possible strategies to support literacy in a UK classroom. This analysis is designed to capture the complexity of literacy development by incorporating multiple stakeholder perspectives, identifying key issues, mapping the interrelationships among factors and outlining strategic options that work holistically within the educational system. It is a valuable way of transforming complex, often ambiguous problems into a structured framework that illuminates the relationship between issues. This is what makes it so useful for the classroom when you are trying to meet the needs of a diverse group (Checkland, 1981).

1. Problem Structuring

This section involves understanding the challenges a practitioner faces when planning their subject to deliver in the classroom.

Possible key challenges to consider:

- Processing
- Attention
- Language and comprehension
- Emotional and social barriers
- Level of knowledge

The first step in developing your thinking in using a SODA map is to think of all the options and use a free thinking exercise such as using Post-It notes to get down all the ideas related to the inquiry. This is best done as a group activity as you'll generate more ideas and gain perspectives which you might not have considered, but it can be done on your own too.

Moment of Reflection 3.14: Curiosity

As you read through the example of using SODA to map options relating to reluctant readers, you might like to explore a current challenging situation in your own setting.

2. Identifying Strategic Options

This section of the plan is best done with Post-It notes and a large wall. Consider ALL the options possible, whether possible in your setting or not. The purpose of this is bigger picture thinking and to get as broad a perspective as possible on the situation. The narrowing down and prioritising comes later.

This might include some of the following:

- Supporting reluctant readers
- Applying specific design principles such as multisensory teaching or **Universal Design for Learning** or **Rosenshine's principles**
- Applying some of the strategies including in this book and creating your own bespoke teaching and learning plan
- Discussing what works with your learners, taking a social approach to learning
- Considering the role of assistive technology in the setting

learner anxiety reading aloud

teacher-led rather than learner-led activities

limited variety in reading activities

ineffective grouping

text too challenging

lack of learner choice in material

limited discussion time

texts too easy

learners distracted easily

learners find reading books boring

limited culturally relevant texts

low learner motivation

too much repetition of same texts

inadequate resources

limited learner input in choosing texts

Figure 3.5 An example of all the options to explore related to reluctant readers

3. Evaluating the Different Approaches

Now is the time to consider what would work best and to rate your chosen options, taking into consideration the following:

Table 3.3 Evaluating a chosen classroom strategy

1. Effectiveness	☆☆☆☆
2. Feasibility	☆☆☆☆
3. Sustainability	☆☆☆☆

When you have identified the best fit for your classroom the next step is to plan the implementation of your chosen approach.

If the options identified in Figure 3.5 are considered and narrowed down to three for the next step in analysis the following questions might be asked:

Option 1: Lack of Learner Choice in Reading Material

This is important because of its direct influence on motivation and autonomy and leads to higher engagement which will in turn reduce classroom disruption.

Option 2: Limited Culturally Relevant Texts

Providing culturally relevant material fosters inclusion, relevance and a stronger connection to reading.

Option 3: Ineffective Grouping

Improved grouping strategies will allow tailored support and enhance the potential for peer learning opportunities. It may lead to less frustration and increase overall engagement.

Table 3.4 Evaluation table of option 1

1. Effectiveness	☆☆☆☆ 4/4 Increased learner choice boosts intrinsic motivation, engagement and reading outcomes.
2. Feasibility	☆☆☆ 3/4 Generally feasible and likely to require only minimal structural changes, though does require resourcing.
3. Sustainability	☆☆☆☆ 4/4 Highly sustainable because once chosen structures are in place, they are easily maintained.

Table 3.5 Evaluation table of option 2

1. Effectiveness	☆☆☆☆ 4/4 Culturally relevant material will likely increase engagement and inclusivity and student identity validation.
2. Feasibility	☆☆ 2/4 May require initial investment in new resources and expertise in choosing suitable texts.
3. Sustainability	☆☆☆ 3/4 Sustainable if there is a commitment to it by the institution and a commitment to maintain and update resources.

Table 3.6 Evaluation table of option 3

1. Effectiveness	☆☆☆ 3/4 Effective in providing differentiated instruction and peer support; however, its success relies heavily on teacher expertise and planning.
2. Feasibility	☆☆ 2/4 Will require continuous teacher training, time-intensive planning and regular monitoring and adjustments.
3. Sustainability	☆☆ 2/4 May be challenging without ongoing support, professional development and consistent monitoring systems which may make it resource intensive.

4. Recommended Strategic Plan

To create a comprehensive, sustainable literacy strategy, a multi-tiered approach is recommended:

Short term (6–12 weeks):

- Introduce strategies which are accessible, affordable and easy to measure progress.
- Provide training on how to use any assistive technology or specific ways of working to all staff and learners who will be using them.
- Share plans with team and department and align approaches with any strategies a learner might have in place already.

Medium term (half an academic year):

- Develop ways of working which are having a noticeable impact.
- Share strategies with parents and other colleagues and advocate for this approach in other subjects or at home.
- Develop a literacy friendly environment for all learners, thinking about delivery and presentation of information as well as resources and aids to support literacy. Begin to embed these practices as your normal way of working.

Long term (a full academic year):

- Develop your approach into a teaching and learning strategy that could be used by others incorporating these short-, medium- and long-term steps, but in addition, be informed by your reflections throughout the process.

- Identify ways in which a learner can become more independent now they are aware of how they learn best and reinforce this way of thinking through stepping back and allowing them space to implement an approach before offering help.
- Become more targeted with support for specific individuals to focus on their specific literacy and build personalised programmes for them that are complemented by your classroom approach.

Moment of Reflection 3.15: Practice

If you have followed along with the above steps, how useful was this as an exercise and will it change what you do when you do what you do?

5. Monitoring and Evaluation

How will you know what is working and what is not?

Keeping a reflective log will help you look back on the progress made in your setting, and at the end of the process consider the following:

1. Learners' progress and development of literacy skills. You might not be the only one to have seen this progress in your setting.
2. Increased confidence and engagement in classroom activities.
3. Your teaching style, increased opportunity for creativity and risk taking.

This strategic approach to identifying the issues and subsequent options enables a broader exploration of what is likely to be a familiar and recurring issue.

The value of this approach can be seen by reflecting on several elements of this chapter:

1. The four areas of need
2. The foundation skill of reading
3. Transdiagnosis

This chapter has progressed through the current areas of need and introduced new ways of thinking about special educational needs and disability.

It has encouraged a reframing of what is already known about learning differences and mental health and shifted the focus to considering the impact of certain skill deficits rather than relying on the separate associated difficulties of a learning difficulty.

This chapter has used the information related to intelligence to reflect upon the opportunities and threats it may present to the other areas of the VSM system and most specifically, planning (system 3) communication (system 2) and production (system 1).

The following Moments of Reflection have been developing your system thinking skills, and in addition to this, you have been encouraged to complete a cognitive map which could directly inform your practice.

Moments of Reflection

- 3.1 Curiosity
- 3.2 Interrelationships
- 3.3 Practice
- 3.4 Multiple Perspective
- 3.5 Practice
- 3.6 Interrelationships
- 3.7 Boundary Judgements
- 3.8 Curiosity
- 3.9 Practice
- 3.10 Interrelationships
- 3.11 Curiosity
- 3.12 Interrelationships
- 3.13 Interrelationships
- 3.14 Curiosity
- 3.15 Practice

References

Adams, R. (2024). England homeschooling surge could become permanent, data suggests. *The Guardian*. www.theguardian.com/education/2024/jan/25/england-homeschooling-surge-could-become-permanent-data-suggests

APA. (2013). *Diagnostic and statistical manual of mental disorders* (5th ed., DSM-5). https://psychiatryonline.org/doi/book/10.1176/appi.books.9780890425596

Ainscow, M., Chapman, C., & Hadfield, M. (2019). *Changing education systems: A research-based approach*. Routledge.

Apperly, I. A., Lee, R., van der Kleij, S. W., & Devine, R. T. (2024). A transdiagnostic approach to neurodiversity in a representative population sample: The N+ 4 model. *JCPP Advances, 4*(2), e12219. doi:10.1002/jcv2.12219.

BBC. (2025). Rising costs force 'difficult choices' on schools. www.bbc.co.uk/news/articles/cy09e7w6jleo

Caspi, A., Houts, R. M., Belsky, D. W., Goldman-Mellor, S. J., Harrington, H., Israel, S., Meier, M. H., Ramrakha, S., Shalev, I., Poulton, R., & Moffitt, T. E. (2014). The p factor: One general psychopathology factor in the structure of psychiatric disorders? *Clinical Psychological Science, 2*(2), 119–137. https://doi.org/10.1177/2167702613497473

CAST. (2024). Universal Design for Learning guidelines, version 3.0. https://udlguidelines.cast.org

Checkland, P. (1981). *Systems thinking, systems practice*. Wiley.

Department of Education. (2024). Education and health care plans: England 2024. www.gov.uk/government/statistics/education-health-and-care-plans-england-2024

Department of Education. (2025). Special educational needs in England: January 2025. https://explore-education-statistics.service.gov.uk/find-statistics/special-educational-needs-in-england/2024-25

Department of Education & Department of Health and Social Care. (2014). SEND Code of Practice: 0 to 25 years. www.gov.uk/government/publications/send-code-of-practice-0-to-25

Department of Education & Department of Health and Social Care. (2022). SEND review: Right support, right place, right time. www.gov.uk/government/consultations/send-review-right-support-right-place-right-time

Ofsted. (2019). *Inspection framework*. https://educationinspection.blog.gov.uk/2019

Ofsted. (2022). *Annual report 2022/23: Education, children's services and skills*. www.gov.uk/government/publications/ofsted-annual-report-202223-education-childrens-services-and-skills

Parliamentary Office of Science and Technology. (2025). Special educational needs and disabilities. POSTnote. https://post.parliament.uk/special-educational-needs-and-disabilities

Scarborough, H. S. (2001). Connecting early language and literacy to later reading (dis)abilities: Evidence, theory, and practice. In S. Neuman & D. Dickinson (Eds), *Handbook for research in early literacy* (pp. 97–110). Guilford Press.

Snyder, H. R., Miyake, A., & Hankin, B. L. (2015). Advancing understanding of executive function impairments and psychopathology: Bridging the gap between clinical and cognitive approaches. *Frontiers in Psychology, 6*, 328. https://doi.org/10.3389/fpsyg.2015.00328

4

A Constellation of Factors Influencing Learning

Overview

This chapter weaves its way through the differences that a learner may have with a specific diagnosis whilst considering several other social and developmental challenges. It recognises the strengths that learners with specific learning differences have and how to draw these out in the classroom developing a strengths-based approach to task planning to run alongside strategies to support difficulties. Not only does it explore specific and detailed differences but also identifies developmental and socio-economic factors which all influence a person's capacity for learning.

The approach used in this chapter takes its inspiration from **Bronfenbrenner's (1979) ecosystem theory** to identify how different factors interrelate. In addition to this, it uses the analogy of a constellation to support the idea that depending on your perspective, constellations can appear more defined or easier to identify, and that the environment plays a significant role in supporting or clouding this view.

At the heart of this theory is the child, who does not grow up in isolation. Every person is shaped by a complex web of relationships, environments and cultural expectations that interact in dynamic but often invisible ways. It is indicative of the 'messy' situation mentioned in previous chapters, where sometimes it is difficult to see where a problem starts and ends. As practitioners when the focus is too narrow on the learner without considering the systems around them, there is a risk of missing the bigger picture regarding behaviour, engagement and learning.

DOI: 10.4324/9781003400639-5

If you have been able to search an image of Bronfenbrenner's model, you will see it is an invitation to foster a wider perspective. It expands and retracts the view around the individual at different levels. The closer the system to the individual, the greater impact but ALL levels can, at times, be the primary driver in a learner's life.

Moment of Reflection 4.1: Interrelationships

As a practitioner reflect on the system around a learner, your role in that system and what the learner's perception of those interrelating systems is and the impact that perspective may have on their learning. For example, a young carer may not see extracurricular activities in the same way as one of their peers.

To support the theories and ideas explored in this book, the first of five case studies will be introduced to outline familiar situations in the classroom from a systems thinking perspective. At the end of the chapter, how cognitive, social and environmental components interrelate to influence learning should be clearer.

Moment of Reflection 4.2: Interrelationships

A causal loop diagram has been provided (see Figure 4.1) to outline the relationships between phonological processing and fluency, but take this one step further and consider the impact on August's co-occurring needs and where on the causal loop diagram her ADHD and dyspraxia might contribute to her challenges with reading?

Case Study 1: A Dyslexic, Dyspraxic, ADHD Learner Struggling with Reading

Background: *August*, a 10-year-old primary school learner.

Diagnoses: Dyslexia, dyspraxia (developmental coordination disorder), and attention deficit hyperactivity disorder (ADHD).

Primary Challenge: August struggles with reading and this is compounded by attention difficulties and coordination issues, making tasks like handwriting, sitting still, and focusing even more challenging.

Impact: August has fallen behind in their reading ability which is affecting their overall academic progress and leading to frustration and low self-esteem.

Key Challenges

Dyslexia

Phonological Processing: August has difficulty decoding words, especially when faced with unfamiliar words or complex spelling patterns. In spite of lots of practice and intervention, their difficulties persist.

Reading Fluency: They read slowly and laboriously, often misreading common words and losing the meaning of the text as they progress. They dislike reading out loud and will avoid this if asked in class.

Spelling and Writing: Spelling is inconsistent, and their difficulty with phonological processing affects their ability to write coherently and keep up with classroom tasks. This is especially noticeable during longer passages

Causal loop diagram highlighting the relationship between phonological skills and the development of fluency.

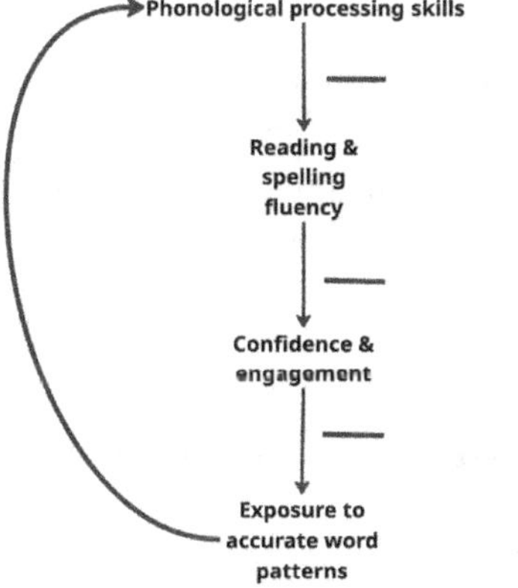

A lack of processing leads to less fluency which leads to a lack of confidence and subsequent lack of exposure to accurate word patterns. This in turn leads to less development of processing skills and the feedback loop continues.

If an intervention for spelling irregular words is carried out, this might improve a learner's spelling ability but because it does not address phonological processing, it will not lead to long term change.

Figure 4.1 A causal loop diagram illustrating the impact of phonological skills on reading and spelling fluency

of text and whilst they may have success in spelling tests, they can't transfer this knowledge to their own writing.

ADHD

Focus and Attention: August finds it hard to concentrate on reading tasks for extended periods, often becoming distracted and losing their place in the text.

Impulsivity: They sometimes guess words or rush through reading, skipping important details, which results in frequent errors.

Restlessness: Sitting still during longer reading sessions is difficult, and they become easily frustrated when tasks require sustained attention.

Dyspraxia/Developmental Coordination Disorder (DCD)

Motor Coordination: Poor hand-eye coordination affects their ability to hold books properly, follow lines of text, and write legibly.

Sequencing Difficulties: August struggles with sequencing tasks, which affects their ability to follow the flow of a story or the order of sentences when reading or writing.

Fine Motor Skills: Slow handwriting and difficulty forming letters impact their ability to take notes or write down key information during reading lessons.

Low Self-Esteem and Motivation

Avoidance Behaviour: Due to repeated struggles, August often avoids reading altogether, resulting in gaps in their literacy development and causing them to fall further behind their peers.

Frustration: Constantly facing challenges with reading has made August feel frustrated and anxious, leading to reduced confidence in their abilities and reluctance to participate in class.

Systems Thinking Approach to Intervention

1. Identifying Key Leverage Points

Multisensory Learning: Given August's learning profile, multisensory approaches which enable August to see, hear and if possible interact with reading and spelling material which will appeal to their interest-led focus. Being multisensory will ensure that it is appealing to both their visual capacity and not relying on their phonological skills as much.

Behavioural Support: Addressing attention issues through ADHD strategies such as structured routines, timed tasks and positive reinforcement to help August stay focused.

Motor Skills Development: Targeting fine motor skills through exercises, such as moving a counter from one finger to another and making a fist and releasing it to activate their hand muscles. Encouraging good posture when reading to accommodate their dyspraxia and make reading tasks more manageable.

2. Developing Intervention Strategies

- **Phonics-Based, Multisensory Approach:**

Using a structured, phonics-based reading programme.

Incorporating auditory elements, such as reading aloud with support (adopting an echo reading strategy), to improve August's phonological awareness and build their ability to decode words.

- **Attention Management and Focus Strategies:**

Chunking Tasks: Breaking down reading tasks into smaller, manageable sections to help August focus for short periods without becoming overwhelmed.

Movement Breaks: Providing regular breaks for movement, allowing August to manage their ADHD-related restlessness while maintaining engagement with reading tasks.

- **Dyspraxia-Friendly Accommodations:**

Assistive Technology: Introducing speech-to-text software and typing programs to help August with written tasks, reducing the physical demands of handwriting.

Gross Motor Activities: Engaging in coordination exercises outside of reading lessons (e.g., ball games, balancing activities) to support overall motor skills development.

Adaptive Tools: Providing slanted reading stands, pencil grips and wider-lined paper to help with posture, book handling, and writing comfort.

- **Building Confidence and Motivation:**

Positive Reinforcement: Using praise and reward systems to celebrate August's reading progress, no matter how small, to help rebuild their confidence.

High-Interest, Low-Reading-Level Books: Providing books on topics that interest August (e.g., animals, space) but are written at a lower reading level to ensure success and enjoyment.

Peer Support: Pairing August with a supportive classmate or reading buddy who can model positive reading habits and provide encouragement.

Classroom Support and Accommodations

1. In-Class Support

One-to-One Reading Intervention: August receives targeted, one-on-one reading support with a specialist or teaching assistant, focusing on phonics and reading fluency. This will support specific targets and allow August to focus in class on the bigger picture and enjoy class readers without the worry of contributing to reading out loud.

Small Group Instruction: Participating in small groups allows August to practice reading with their peers in a low-pressure setting, improving their confidence and engagement.

Differentiated Instruction: Practitioners adapt reading assignments to August's needs, providing extra time to complete tasks and adjusting expectations for written work.

2. Use of Technology

Audiobooks: Introducing audiobooks as a way for August to access content and stories that are above their independent reading level, helping them build comprehension while reducing frustration with decoding.

Text-to-Speech Software: Allowing August to use software that reads text aloud, enabling them to follow along while hearing the correct pronunciation and flow of the text.

3. Reading Environment

Quiet, Distraction-Free Space: Ensuring August has a calm, organised space for reading, free from distractions, to help them focus on the task at hand.

Fidget Tools: Providing fidget tools or stress balls to help manage their restlessness without disrupting the learning environment.

4. Parental Involvement

Home Reading Routine: Practitioners collaborate with August's parents to establish a consistent, enjoyable reading routine at home, including audiobooks and shared reading activities.

Open Communication: Regular communication between school and home to monitor August's progress and adjust interventions as necessary.

Moment of Reflection 4.3: Practice

Reflect on the suggestions made here for classroom support. Are there any you currently employ? What, if any, might you adapt for your setting?

What would the impact be of this change?

Outcomes

1. Improved Reading Skills

Through structured phonics instruction and multisensory learning techniques, August begins to improve their decoding skills and reading fluency. They are better able to sound out words and recognise common sight words, leading to increased reading comprehension.

With the help of assistive technology, August can complete reading tasks more independently, reducing their frustration with decoding and improving their ability to follow along with lessons.

2. Enhanced Focus and Attention

The use of chunked reading tasks and regular movement breaks helps August stay focused for longer periods, allowing them to complete reading assignments without becoming overwhelmed.

3. Increased Confidence and Engagement

As August experiences small successes in reading, their confidence grows. They are more willing to engage with reading tasks in class and at home, showing a renewed interest in books and stories.

The use of high-interest, low-level reading materials motivates August to practice reading independently, and their anxiety around reading tasks decreases.

4. Improved Motor Coordination and Writing

With support from an occupational therapist and the use of assistive tools, August's handwriting improves, and they can complete written tasks more efficiently.

The fine motor skill exercises and adaptations (e.g., pencil grips, typing programs) reduce their frustration with writing and allow them to focus more on the content of their reading and writing tasks.

5. Reduced Anxiety and Frustration

August's avoidance behaviour decreases as they feel more supported and successful in reading. Their anxiety about falling behind in class is reduced, and they begin to participate more actively in reading and writing activities.

The positive reinforcement and peer support help August feel more included and capable, reducing their sense of isolation and frustration in the classroom.

Moment of Reflection 4.4: Multiple Perspectives

There are several stakeholders mentioned in this case study. How do you ensure that August's voice is central to the support that is recommended for them?

Current Definitions of Specific Learning Difficulties

The following specific learning difficulties are listed in the **Diagnostic and Statistical Manual of Mental Disorders, Fifth Edition (DSM-5)** and are specific as opposed to general because they are all on a spectrum and don't affect a person's ability to learn in all areas. As research advances our understanding of these difficulties changes are made, for example attention deficit disorder (ADD) has been replaced by ADHD and Asperger's is no longer recognised as separate from autism spectrum condition. Similarly, as will be explained later in this chapter, the definition of dyslexia has recently been under review as has the definition of dyscalculia.

At the end of each section is a positive perspective on the specific learning difficulty and what might be harnessed in the classroom to boost the learner's confidence.

Attention Deficit Hyperactivity Disorder (ADHD)

ADHD is a neurodevelopmental difficulty that can be characterised by persistent challenges with inattention, hyperactivity and/or impulsivity. As the understanding of ADHD grows with the increasing numbers of people becoming diagnosed, how it affects the person, rather than just how they focus on their surroundings, is of importance. ADHD has only been diagnosed in adults since 2008, and the DSM-5 definition was broadened to include organisation and time management. In addition to this, more research has been carried out into associated difficulties that impact working relationships and productivity.

Novel Ideas and Energising Company

An ADHD learner will bring energy, spirit and a thirst for knowledge to the classroom. They will enjoy exploring ideas creatively and if they're interested, they will be able to focus and sustain a level of concentration which blocks out all other distractions. They are dynamic thinkers and quick problem solvers.

Sam Reynolds is an experienced ADHD assessor who has worked in multidisciplinary teams both supporting and diagnosing ADHD. She explains below the key factors of ADHD and how to support both adults and children.

Dear practitioner,

What is ADHD?

To receive a diagnosis of ADHD, a child must have difficulties in two or more settings, their difficulties must be causing a moderate impairment socially, academically or otherwise, and symptoms must be persistent. Practitioners and school staff are often in a unique position to identify learners with ADHD symptoms and recognise the signs early, limiting the impact symptoms might have on academia and self-esteem, so creating understanding, inclusive environments that support needs is crucial.

Children with ADHD might:

- *have lots of energy and find it hard to sit still*
- *struggle to concentrate or keep focused on a task unless it's something they really enjoy, and even then they may get frustrated because they just can't stay on task and do it*
- *get bored easily and become distracted or daydream*
- *find it hard to remember instructions*
- *forget to do homework or bring items into school, take things home – or out of their bags*
- *lose things, be disorganised and untidy*
- *find it hard to carry out tasks which involve waiting or taking turns*
- *distract other people by speaking or making noises or being hyperactive*
- *interrupt conversations and/or blurt out answers, not wait in queues or compete when finishing things*
- *say or act impulsively, perhaps being regretful after the fact*
- *have a reputation for being a troublemaker or hard to manage.*

ADHD can present differently for each individual and challenges can be long-lasting and affect education, relationships and mental health.

Education

- *ADHD does not indicate low intelligence (though SpLDs are often diagnosed alongside it), but it can limit academic potential and attainment.*
- *Underachievement can impact confidence and self-esteem and learners may feel stupid, or like they can never do what they're supposed to.*

Relationships

People with ADHD can struggle to regulate their emotions, which can lead to outbursts. Being impulsive and neglecting social cues can make it hard to maintain positive relationships.

Mental health/well-being

Frequent rejection, failing at tasks and causing problems can affect confidence, and cause anxiety and depression.

Those with ADHD may feel isolated/rejected because of their outbursts – or because other people may think they are strange or different.

What is helpful for children with ADHD?

ADHD medicines work by affecting the levels of neurotransmitters in the brain which help regulate attention. School feedback on the effects of medicine will be instrumental in ensuring that the right medicine and the right dose are used for each
individual.

Rules, discipline and support

- *Boundaries should be clear and consistent, across classes and subjects, and consequences should be proportionate and immediate. You'll need to be patient and respond with kindness and calmness – some learners with ADHD need clear warnings and/or instructions repeated.*
- *Seating plans: Inattentive learners tend to do better if they are sat at the front of class and can be prompted/reminded and see instructions on the board. Use their name when speaking to ensure they are listening or to regain attention.*

- *Minimise distractions: Consider where the learner is sat, away from windows or doors and potentially not near others with similar difficulties.*
- *Workload: Break down workloads into smaller, more manageable (and memorable) chunks or write/draw instructions or use flowcharts and make sure work is set at an appropriate level – neither too hard or too easy, and make it creative to keep interest.*
- *Tools, equipment and adjustments: Pupils may need a fidget toy or sensory/ behavioural equipment to aid concentration, otherwise they will find other things to distract themselves.*
- *Forcing oneself to concentrate can be exhausting so if permissible, allow extra time for rest or movement breaks to manage stress and fatigue.*
- *Give feedback: Positive and negative feedback should be given in real time – those with ADHD find it particularly difficult to defer rewards and often need encouragement to continue on, especially if they've struggled for a while and have low self-esteem.*

Best wishes,
Sam

Moment of Reflection 4.5: Practice

What assumptions do I hold about learners who struggle with inattention and impulsivity?

Does my classroom practice promote connection and self-worth for all learners, including those that struggle to regulate attention or emotion?

Dyslexia

Dyslexia is a lifelong condition that is not caused by a lack of intelligence or motivation. The British Dyslexia Association (2018) reports that approximately 10% of people in the UK are affected by dyslexia. Dyslexia is a learning difficulty that primarily affects the skills involved in accurate and fluent word reading and spelling. Characteristic features of dyslexia are

Table 4.1 Current definitions of dyslexia

Source	*Definition*
International Dyslexia Association (2002)	Dyslexia is a specific learning disability that is neurobiological in origin. It is characterised by difficulties with accurate and/or fluent word recognition and by poor spelling and decoding abilities. These difficulties typically result from a deficit in the phonological component of language that is often unexpected in relation to other cognitive abilities and effective classroom instruction. Secondary consequences may include problems in reading comprehension and reduced reading experience that can impede growth of vocabulary and background knowledge.
Rose Review (2009)	Dyslexia is a learning difficulty that primarily affects the skills involved in accurate and fluent word reading and spelling. Characteristic features of dyslexia are difficulties in phonological awareness, verbal memory and verbal processing speed. Dyslexia occurs across the range of intellectual abilities. It is best thought of as a continuum, not a distinct category, and there are no clear cut-off points. Co-occurring difficulties may be seen in aspects of language, motor coordination, mental calculation, concentration and personal organisation, but these are not, by themselves, markers of dyslexia. A good indication of the severity and persistence of dyslexic difficulties can be gained by examining how the individual responds or has responded to well-founded intervention.
DSM 5 Definition (APA, 2013)	Dyslexia is included under 'Specific Learning Disorder' (SLD). It is diagnosed when a person has difficulties with word reading accuracy, reading rate or fluency, and reading comprehension, which are persistent despite intervention. The condition is neurobiological in origin and typically manifests as problems with decoding and spelling, affecting educational performance. It is persistent across the lifespan and may co-occur with other neurodevelopment differences such as ADHD and DCD (dyspraxia). The impact varies depending on environmental and educational factors.
Delphi Consensus Definition (Carroll et al., 2025)	Dyslexia is a set of processing difficulties that affect the acquisition of reading and spelling. The most commonly observed cognitive impairment in dyslexia is a difficulty in phonological processing (i.e., in phonological awareness, phonological processing speed or phonological memory). However, phonological difficulties do not fully explain the variability that is observed. Working memory, processing speed and orthographic skills can contribute to the impact of dyslexia.

difficulties in phonological awareness, verbal memory and verbal processing speed. These difficulties can cause problems with reading comprehension and spelling. Dyslexia, as it is not considered a medical condition like ADHD or autism has a DSM-5 classification, but this definition is not used widely in the UK. There are a few definitions which are used by assessors, but specialist assessors are advised to use the most recent.

Moment of Reflection 4.6: Curious

How does having more than one definition of something impact it? Does it allow for more scope in terms of definition, or does it somehow undermine it?

The definition of dyslexia has always posed a problem for society. Never mind the individuals that gain diagnosis. Firstly, it began as a difficulty, which was measured by assessing a person's intelligence. This was known as the deficit model, suggesting that a lower intelligence score (visual and/or verbal ability) did not qualify someone as dyslexic but having low literacy. People with a lower visual or verbal ability were classed as low literacy rather than dyslexic. Elliot and Grigorenko (2014) argued whether dyslexia exists at all and that its existence means those that struggle with literacy are missing out on support if they fail to receive a diagnosis.

One Delphi study of dyslexia (Carroll, 2025) incorporates risk factors. Below are examples of risk factors:

Familial History: A significant risk factor for dyslexia is a family history of the condition, indicating a genetic component.

Speech or Language Difficulties in Early Childhood: Children who experience speech or language difficulties before starting school are at an increased risk of developing literacy challenges, including dyslexia.

Cognitive Factors: Impairments in areas such as working memory, attention control, processing speed, and phonological processing can contribute to the development of dyslexia.

Environmental Influences: Factors such as the quality of reading instruction, the home literacy environment, and socio-economic status can play a role in how significant their dyslexia or literacy difficulties are.

Visual Thinkers and Creative Communicators

A dyslexic learner will often be adept at verbal communication; they are able to visualise situations and problems drawing on images to aid their memory. They are verbal storytellers and often good actors, artists and entrepreneurs. As much of their time has been spent in environments which don't suit them (a literacy-based education system), they develop resilience, tenacity and their own ways of working in order to make progress.

The following insight is from Kate Paterson, a practitioner in an international school who is open about her dyslexia and the impact on her role as a practitioner. As a member of her school senior leadership team, she is in a position to shape the way the school approaches learning differences and understand what support or understanding is needed for both the practitioners and learners to thrive.

Dear Reader,

A phrase I got used to hearing growing up was, 'Katie has dyslexia', and I would watch the practitioners around me process what that meant. I understood that it was an important part of my identity that my parents needed to share with my schools so they could, hopefully, best support me. I think my educational journey led me to teaching because I always wanted to make a difference for other young learners. I could have let my dyslexia diagnosis consume me, but my parents made sure to celebrate what I could do while still acknowledging the challenges.

Being a practitioner with dyslexia and living out my dream of teaching is so fulfilling (I had to type that word six times before the computer caught up with me!). I feel fortunate that I can see learning through a different lens, which lets me support and connect with my learners in unique ways. When a learner is struggling to read, recall something, or when I see their brains moving a mile a minute, my first thought is, 'How can I support them but also celebrate them?' I don't want them to feel that they have to just cope or mask how they are feeling.

That is not to say that being a practitioner and having dyslexia is easy. I still struggle with a lot of the written elements, and I used to worry so much about making mistakes in front of people – what if they realised I'd been hiding? I remember, in my first few years of teaching, I was writing down learners' ideas on the board, and I spelled something wrong. They noticed, and I panicked for a moment. I started to question how I could make it better and ended up doing the best thing without intending to: I modelled making a mistake, asking for help, and trying again. That's all we need to be successful – try, ask for help if you don't understand, and when you're ready, try again.

I recently talked to our Year 6 cohort about having dyslexia, and it was the most rewarding session I've done. They asked such interesting questions about how it affected me emotionally and how I manage now. The group was so accepting, which speaks volumes. We have to share our experiences and connect so others can understand.

This year, I've transitioned into a bigger leadership role, and one of my main goals is to talk more openly with our neurodivergent staff about their strengths. For there to be a culture of acceptance, there needs to be a strong understanding of who we are as a learning community. Awareness, understanding and support are key factors for me when trying to create a kind and inclusive shared learning environment.

From Kate Paterson,
Assistant Principal and PYP Coordinator

Moment of Reflection 4.7: Interrelationships

How open and supportive is your setting to staff who share they are neurodivergent?

Dyscalculia and/or Maths Difficulties

A recent review of maths difficulties has seen the introduction of two different specific learning difficulty (SpLD) classifications. These are recognised and endorsed by the SpLD Assessment Standards Committee (SASC):

1. SpLD maths difficulties are defined as a persistent challenge with learning and applying mathematical skills. These may arise from a range of underlying causes including difficulties with working memory, language, attention or visual-spatial processing.
2. SpLD dyscalculia is defined as affecting the ability to acquire arithmetical skills. Learners may have difficulty understanding number concepts, performing accurate and fluent calculations, or understanding and using numbers or mathematical symbols (SASC, n.d.).

Therefore an individual could receive a standalone diagnosis in one of these or alongside other co-occurring specific learning difficulties.

Learners with maths difficulties.

Dyscalculia is less common than maths difficulties.

Challenges with numeracy may also be explored in a dyslexia assessment in relation to the literacy load of mathematics and the impact that dyslexia may have on the subject. For example, being able to answer wordy problems or scenarios with several elements.

Dyscalculia or maths difficulties can be mistaken for maths anxiety, but they are not the same. Maths anxiety is a fear of maths that can be caused by a number of factors, including negative experiences with math in the past or a lack of confidence in one's mathematical abilities.

Dyscalculia or maths difficulties may include challenges with the following:

- Understanding numbers and their relationships to each other
- Memorising basic maths facts
- Performing basic maths calculations
- Understanding and applying mathematical concepts
- Solving maths problems
- Copying numbers accurately
- Reading and writing numbers

Adept Problem Solvers

Learners with maths difficulties often have innovative and practical skills in problem solving and are strong verbal communicators. They are often adept at processing complex ideas and simplifying them for others.

Dyspraxia or DCD

Dyspraxia/DCD is a common difficulty that affects movement and coordination. It is a neurological condition that affects the way the brain processes information about movement. This can lead to problems with balance, coordination and fine motor skills.

Dyspraxia/DCD is not caused by any single factor, but it is thought to be due to a combination of genetic and environmental factors. It is estimated that 5–10% of learners have dyspraxia, and it is more common in boys than girls (Blank et al., 2019; Li et al., 2024).

The challenges of dyspraxia/DCD can vary from person to person, but they may include:

- Poor balance
- Difficulty with some sports and other physical activities
- Problems with handwriting
- Difficulty with dressing and undressing
- Problems with time management and organisation
- Difficulty with social skills
- Poor **proprioception** (knowing where your limbs and body are in relation to the space around it)

Empathetic and Resilient Leaders

Dyspraxic learners may have faced adversity and developed tenacity to keep practising skills which many take for granted. They often have strengths in conceptualising ideas and visualising outcomes, especially when supported to identify individual steps and sequences. They might have a strong appreciation for colour, music and abstract patterns. They are strong verbal communicators and can often identify alternative ways to solve problems.

Developmental Language Disorder (DLD)

Developmental language disorder (DLD) is a developmental difficulty characterised by difficulties with language acquisition and use despite normal non-verbal intelligence and no obvious neurological or sensory impairments. Learners with DLD typically experience delays or deficits in understanding and producing spoken language, which can affect various aspects of their learning and communication skills.

Impact on learning:

- Academic achievement: DLD can significantly affect a learner's academic performance, particularly in subjects that require strong language skills, such as reading, writing and comprehension of verbal instructions.
- Social interaction: Difficulties with language can also impact a learner's social interactions, making it challenging for them to communicate

effectively with peers, form friendships and participate in group activities.

- Self-esteem: DLD learners may experience frustration and low self-esteem due to their struggles with language, especially if they perceive themselves as different from their peers or face difficulties in expressing themselves.

Intuitive and Visual Thinkers

In terms of strengths, DLD learners can be excellent readers of other forms of communication, and can be sensitive and intuitive as well as good listeners. When confident and empowered, they can be measured and seek clarification about ideas leading to less misunderstandings. They may excel in visual tasks, with a good eye for detail and pattern recognition. They can have good long-term memory skills and be hands-on learners.

Autism

Autism shows up differently in everyone, but there are some unifying traits.

Social communication:

- Finding it tricky to read social cues and body language
- Taking things literally rather than understanding hidden meanings
- Having a direct communication style that some might find too honest
- Struggling with small talk or unstructured social situations

Sensory experiences:

- Being more sensitive to sounds, lights, textures or smells than others
- Getting overwhelmed in busy or noisy environments
- Having strong preferences for certain textures in food or clothing

Routines and interests:

- Having interests in specific topics
- Finding comfort in routines and predictability
- Finding changes challenging, especially when unexpected

Processing information:

- Needing more time to process verbal information
- Finding it helpful to have written instructions
- Getting exhausted from social interactions and needing alone time to recharge

Remember: These traits aren't 'problems' to be fixed – they're just different ways of experiencing and interacting with the world.

Detailed-Focused Organisers

An autistic learner may be detail-oriented, reliable and hard working. They will offer depth to problem solving and challenge to processes if seen as flawed. They can be visual thinkers with skills in problem solving that require logic and sequencing.

Moment of Reflection 4.8: Curiosity

Nikki mentions a few theories in this letter. Evaluate your familiarity with these theories and whether you would benefit from finding out more about them.

This contribution is from an autism specialist and perpetual learner, Nikki Read. It embodies curiosity but also passion and commitment to supporting neurodiverse people. Nikki has experience of diagnosing autism, raising neurodivergent learners and educating others about their neurodiversity. She has identified the key considerations when supporting someone with autism but her perspective embraces systems thinking.

Dear practitioner,

After the initial intrigue at what I might want to share with a practitioner as they explore how best to support an autistic child, trainee, pupil, or perhaps educate a colleague, the enormity of this task really hit home.

What nuggets of information can I share to make life just a little easier for the practitioner and recipient?

Autism is such a broad presentation of characteristics. We are regularly reminded of the unique presentation each individual will bring to your setting and, of course, it is likely to be one of a potential cluster of differences, or neurodivergence, unique to that individual.

There is also the ever-changing landscape of terminology before even contemplating the vast array of potential scaffolds and support mechanisms. Autism exists within an especially political frame and 'warrior' parents are often battle worn and vocal in their requests for their learners. Adding further to the complexity, you may not see an autistic presentation. Very often autism is wrapped within a performance of 'typical' behaviour so extensive that the authentic autistic identity becomes lost, requiring careful support in later life to unravel. Underpinning all of this is the practitioner juggling to meet the needs of every other learner, curriculum requirements, national outcome statistics, marking, record keeping and all of the usual busyness of daily life within education.

I get it. Having worked in various guises within education for around 19 years, supporting autistic learners and adults, running after school clubs for the National Autistic Society, creating and delivering psycho education, working and studying as a neurodivergent mother and, most importantly, being a parent of autistic twins, I really do get it. Planning for, and accommodating, a unique, complex and invisible neurotype is not an easy task. The NHS cites research that between 10% and 20% of the world's population is neurodivergent. That means approximately 3–6 pupils in a class of 30 will fall into this category, whether that be dyslexia, ADHD, autism etc. If you are delivering training to a university cohort of 40 learners, how do you factor in the mechanisms to meet their diverse needs and accommodate their unique strengths? And this within an era where services are quite literally creaking under the pressure of demand and with pools of funding drying up in real time.

There are some 'golden guides' that you might want to explore. Whilst they are written with an autistic learner at the forefront, they work for so many neurodivergent presentations. Simply put, they are good practice in any educational setting. They will not work for every learner, but they will hopefully be supportive of the majority.

Golden guide 1 – *Trust the paperwork. I have overheard many conversations in staff rooms disputing the lengthy reports that often arrive with learners. Whilst the media can allude to the ease of an 'off the shelf' diagnosis, this is extremely rare. An autism assessment is long, upsetting and requires a unique* *set of skills the assessor develops through extensive training and hours of clinical experience, and is based upon the use of a series of tools, interviews with an informant and the individual, and through careful clinical observation, bound under stringent diagnostic criteria and within the NICE Guidance (n.d.). I undertake assessments as part of a team. An assessment can involve anywhere between a minimum of two people or a team of five or six, including psychiatrists and speech and language therapists. An average autism assessment will take around 8–10 hours, and that is when it is 'straightforward'.*

Golden guide 2 – *Stay current. There is an obligation for local authorities to provide training in autism and a wealth of guest speakers just waiting on an invite to an INSET day. But let's be realistic, practitioners are time poor and generally do not dictate the CPD/INSET itinerary. Plus, how to remember all of the amazing gems of knowledge when added into the latest STEM or curriculum guidance for schools, safeguarding updates etc. A quick search of 'current theories on autistic presentation' using a search engine highlighted the following: a strength-based neurodiversity approach, which introduced the double empathy theory (Milton, 2012) and intense world theory, and discussed executive functioning, cognitive and motor/coordination differences. There are limitations; mono-tropism (Murray et al., 1995) was not mentioned and is essential in understanding the single channel processing of an autistic individual, but summary research is for when you are in a bind and pressed for time. Maybe try a podcast whilst out for a run or cooking tea. Or, and this can really help with building bridges, ask your parents or local support groups for the top three authors or podcasters they would recommend you listen to. I appreciate the workload is higher, but you'll have a deeper understanding of the influences on your learner and their primary caregivers.*

Golden guide 3 – *Think environment. Bright and colourful classrooms, busy labs or lecture halls are wonderful, unless you have a hypersensitivity to visual processing. Your array of beautiful bangles or the heel taps on your shoes may become all a learner can hear. A low arousal setting is ideal for our learners. Understanding the influence of the sensory world allows us to remove some of the barriers to learning. Have a colourful corner or facilitate inclusion with noise cancelling headphones during a loud activity, perhaps explore establishing a quiet space. The less sensory information an autistic individual must process means the less likely they are to become overwhelmed. It will also highlight instances of sensory seeking behaviours, for example movement seeking, touching their neighbours' pens and pencils or chewing their sleeves.*

We can use these to kickstart their executive functioning. For example, a resistance band across the front legs of a chair affords some proprioceptive and vestibular sensory processing and is likely to engage learning. I have heard many practitioners (and parents) state that autistic learners are going to have to live in the 'real world'. Yes, they are but that is also a world where the need for these adjustments is recognised and supported under legislation as reasonable adjustments. Building a picture of the unique sensory profile your learner brings to the table can help us to mitigate sensory overwhelm or understimulation, reducing meltdowns in all settings and removing barriers to learning.

***Golden guide 4** – User-friendly strategies. Be direct and explicit. Use clear language and back it up with visuals. We've known for many years now the challenges an autistic learner can face in trying to follow a lesson or task whilst also attempting to translate metaphors, sarcasm and social language that feels obscure and alien. Add into this the additional demand of trying to offer eye-gaze, sit still and stifle sensory pulls such as tapping and fidgeting. Chunk tasks and think about backward chaining. Yes, it's more work but this can be a great scaffold for autism, ADHD, dyslexia, dyspraxia and learners with processing differences. Once resources are created, you have them ready to go for the next learner who may benefit. An autistic learner may take in much more information if we also reduce the social and sensory demands placed upon them. Group learning is not for all. Explore how learning feels most comfortable and then work to that strength where we can.*

***Golden guide 5** – Maintain a routine and predictable environment. That does not mean that everything must remain the same, more that we need to understand and be prepared for the impact of changes and transitions. A change of practitioner, new display, change of subject – all can cause anxiety for an autistic learner. This may be internalised and exhibit later at home as a meltdown or it may be externalised in the setting, perhaps appearing as defiance, rudeness or hitting another learner. Warnings in advance or time to transition and adjust with a regulating activity might help. Try to remember that a change is a change; even where it might be fun the influence on an autistic neurotype is the same. A simple transition warning 'literacy in five minutes', 'lunch break in two minutes' can lift the load on an autistic individual. When you live in a world that rarely makes sense and that feels unpredictable, familiarity and routine are key.*

Golden guide 6** – Think double empathy. Differences in communication, interests and reciprocity are very much a two-way problem. Autism is a neurotype based on neurobiological differences. These differences result in misunderstandings between the autistic individual and the non-autistic* *individual. An autistic learner may struggle to understand the thoughts and feelings of others. A non-autistic individual may struggle to understand the thoughts and feelings of an autistic individual; the miscommunication highway runs both ways. We can respect the preferences of the individual and accommodate where possible. But we also need to teach how to navigate social interaction and allow ourselves to be taught. What is not ok is for an individual, autistic or otherwise, to feel slighted or abused by the behaviour of another. Being autistic does not mean a learner can do or say whatever they feel, in the same way that being neurotypical or allistic does not mean our interaction style is the only way to interact. Being curious and empathetic to the experiences of autistic learners opens up a world of validation for them and an incredible insight for us. For example, 36% of autistic people experience the world with face blindness* ***(prosopagnosia) *compared with 6% of people without autism. Can you imagine what that must be like? To not be able to recognise facial expressions, to recognise someone by their haircut or colour? We cannot understand these challenges without curiosity and empathetic exploration. How hard must it be for a pupil to turn up in class, but their practitioner no longer looks like their practitioner because they had a haircut and beard trim?*

Golden guide 7 *– The power of positivity. Autism is a neurotype; as such the differences are present due to what we minimally understand as structural and genetic variations. This is also true for ADHD, dyspraxia etc. If a learner is overwhelmed to the point of meltdown, a missed play time or detention is not the fix. Explore positive approaches where possible (yes, I know, there are occasions when there is no choice but to implement a 'cause and effect' stance). Reward strengths, recognise when an individual achieves, allow for processing time to encourage the learner. Be flexible in delivery and work together to create a toolkit of proactive strategies. These may include movement breaks, sensory breaks, low arousal activities. This works for all learners. A learner stressed by missing a submission deadline that has also been unable to eat in the noisy canteen is less likely to absorb key information in a lecture. A message or email to recognise the sterling job of actually arriving in class and a reminder of how they can utilise their incredible analytical skills to compare the merits of CBT vs DBT may be enough to help them take a deep breath and get back on track. A sharp criticism or 'stick' will not develop the neurobiological changes required to enhance executive functioning or improve working memory.*

Golden guide 8 *– Collaborate. Many years ago, an educational psychologist said to me that autistic parents are the hardest and least tolerant parents* *they have ever had to work with – not the most helpful comment. She then explained that this is because of the inherent exhaustion of trying to become experts on their child, fight for health services and fight to get the education their learner deserves. All this within the context of sleep deprivation, and having their parenting explored under the microscope of education, social care and health/mental health. Work with families, learners, specialists; with a cohesive team behind them your learner really will fly towards achieving their potential. Join with parents in hammering down closed doors, seek training, ask what works at home. In my home, these are the practitioners that my adult sons still talk about, generally with minds full of admiration and laughter but always with hearts full of love. Most importantly collaborate with your learner. Explore together what makes for a good day of learning; what does that look like and feel like? Rate strategies, build a toolkit, teach each other.*

Apply the PACE approach to our teaching.

Playful, Acceptance, Curiosity and Empathy.

As people, we cannot like everyone we come across nor can we be experts in everything. What we can do is afford opportunity by growing our understanding and creating environments that welcome in autistic learners with open minds and open hearts through allowing them to learn in spaces and with practitioners that help them to feel safe and to celebrate their unique selves.

Best wishes,
Nikki Read
Autism/Neurodiversity Practitioner

Moment of Reflection 4.9: Practice

Choose one or two of Nicky's golden guides to focus on in your practice and monitor the impact of them over a set period of time.

Shared Traits of Specific Learning Difficulties

All the specific learning difficulties discussed in this section share the following cognitive difficulties, which in turn, can all impact learning.

However, the following shared traits can all be supported through targeted interventions.

1. **Executive functioning:** This starts with being able to direct attention to the task in hand rather than it being hijacked by something else, for example intrusive thoughts, sensory information or emotions. This will also impact organisation, time management and being ready to learn.
2. **Working memory:** This will make it harder to follow instructions, process verbal and written information and may make reading and writing slower.
3. **Processing differences:** These can be differences in processing; some learners can be fast verbal processors but slow processes when it comes to written information. They may show skills in processing words but are then slower to comprehend that information. Fast decoders but slow comprehenders. For an autistic learner this may be due to the content but for a dyslexic learner it may be the letters and words themselves which causes them to be slower.
4. **Language and communication differences:** This could be breadth of vocabulary, difficulties in understanding or making themselves understood. It could be the structure of the information or the complexity.

If the above skills require **scaffolding** and all are explored in the following chapter, there are common strengths too and planning support which makes the most of these enables **neurodivergent** learners to thrive.

1. **Resilience:** Every neurodivergent learner should be commended for their resilience as they will have experienced difficulties from the beginning of their education, and they are still turning up every day to do hard things.
2. **Creative problem solving and innovation:** Often if you learn in a different way to others, you have a different perspective on things, and this can often enlighten and enrich tasks and conversations.
3. **Pattern recognition and visual acuity:** Being able to see connections between seemingly unrelated things and visualising situations has been proven to be a strength of many neurodivergent learners.

Increasing the opportunities for these learners to develop these skills and, more importantly, demonstrate them allows them to take the lead in tasks and gives them a much-needed confidence boost.

Applying a Strengths-Based Approach in Practice

Task

Design an ecofriendly school garden.

A group of four neurodivergent learners collaborate on a project which works to their strengths.

Strength →Role

1. Attention to detail and precision and research skills → Research and design
2. Idea generation, enthusiasm and energy → Project facilitator
3. Visualisation, verbal communication → Storytelling and community engagement
4. Spatial awareness, organisation, logic → Practical implementation leader

The Interconnections Between the Skills

- Precision of the research informs the practical implementation of the task.
- The energy provided by the project facilitator enables everyone to work together and quick thinking ensures that any concerns are dealt with swiftly.
- The creative storytelling ensures engagement with the community and draws interest from the outset.

Moment of Reflection 4.10: Curiosity

Before you begin to consider literacy, which plays a role in every subject, reflect on the literacy load of a subject. This could be the vocabulary, is it subject related or does it include unfamiliar words which will need explaining? Does it demand a specific approach to answering questions which again might need teaching explicitly?

Literacy Development

Below the age of seven most skills are dependent on that learner's rate of development, and it is difficult to measure whether a learner is struggling because of a specific difficulty or that they will genuinely catch-up given time. However, the earlier you intervene with a learner who is struggling, the more successful you will be in teaching the foundation skills needed to progress through a frantically paced curriculum.

As a learner progresses through the years at school it is difficult to ever revisit the alphabet or the basic letter sounds. If spelling rules like split **digraphs** and double **consonants** in words are not stuck like glue in a learner's mind, they are unlikely to be repeated enough as they move on to more complex grammatical structures and that learner will continue to make the same errors throughout their education.

Signs That a Learner May Be Struggling with Literacy

While there is no definitive list to identify a learner who is struggling with literacy, there are some signs that you may be able to pick up on if your learner is finding reading and writing tricky.

- Have you noticed or received comments from your child's practitioner that their written work does not match what they are verbally capable of?
- Do they know all the answers during a discussion but then lack detail, accuracy and content when they write it down?
- Can they use complex vocabulary when talking about their ideas, but their written work features simple, easy to spell alternatives?
- Can they read or spell a word correctly one week but then have completely forgotten it the following week?
- When they read, are they looking for clues in the pictures and making incorrect predictions about unfamiliar words?
- Do they need more time than feels comfortable for you to think about their answers to verbal or written questions?
- Are they considered poor listeners and disorganised but have a great memory for landmarks or people's faces?

Key Stage 2 – Less Skill Building and Increased Application

There is an assumption that most learners will have acquired the basic literacy skills of phonological awareness (the knowledge of sounds in words), built sight word knowledge and read with a good level of automaticity.

Similarly, their writing skills should be fluent and writing individual words should not take much brain power; more energy should be directed to the content they are writing and developing their voice and writing style.

When a learner reaches 8.5/9 and they continue to struggle with reading or writing fluency, this is the time to monitor and intervene with high-quality interventions. Some recommendations are included in Chapter 7.

What to Monitor in a Learner in Key Stage 2

- Inconsistencies with their reading, word-attack and spelling skills.
- Disparity between their verbal and written ability. Their spoken answers are more developed and include varied vocabulary in comparison to their written answers.
- If they find it hard to get going with their work when working independently.
- They may find it hard to follow more than two instructions.
- They start to see a difference in their ability compared to their friends and it is affecting their confidence.
- Whether they need more time to process instructions, read and get their ideas down on paper.

The Transition to Secondary Education

The transition from a primary to a secondary setting marks a significant shift in both environment and expectations for learners and this can be a steep learning curve for some and too steep if the scaffolds aren't there from either the school or home during this time.

A learner's experience of transition can impact their entire time in secondary education, so it is important to get it right.

A learner arriving in Year 7 is expected to have the following literacy skills:

1. Read fluently and with comprehension.
2. Write coherently for a range of purposes and audiences.
3. Apply accurate and varied vocabulary.
4. Spell with fluency most high and medium frequency words as well as be able to apply their knowledge of spelling rules and phonological skills to spell new words correctly.
5. Express their ideas both verbally and on paper with varied vocabulary and syntax, and use language with purpose.

Moment of Reflection 4.11: Multiple Perspectives

What is your experience of upper primary and/or Year 7 learners? Broaden your perspective on this by discussing it with your peers. What is your learned experience of the biggest challenge when learners transition from primary to secondary education?

Adolescence: A Time Comparable to the First 12 Months of Life in Terms of Brain Development

Whilst this book is clear on its intentions to support those who find learning a challenge, it would be remiss not to acknowledge the huge impact that puberty has on a young person.

Adolescence is a time of huge brain changes that shape how young people think, learn and make decisions. These changes can sometimes make learning feel challenging, but they also offer incredible opportunities for growth.

Key Brain Changes and Their Impact on Learning

*Thinking and Decision Making (**Prefrontal Cortex** Growth)*

The part of the brain responsible for planning, problem solving and self-control is still developing at this point. This means teenagers may struggle with organisation, managing time or thinking ahead, but they're also learning to reason and make decisions more independently.

*Emotions and Risk-Taking (**Limbic System** Activity)*

The emotional centre of the brain develops faster than the thinking part, which explains why teens can be impulsive or strongly influenced by their feelings and peers. Learning works best when it's engaging, relevant and connected to real-world experiences.

Brain Efficiency (Pruning and Strengthening Connections)

The brain strengthens important pathways and gets rid of unused ones. This means practice and repetition help solidify learning. Teenagers benefit from hands-on, interactive learning that makes information stick.

*Motivation and Rewards (**Dopamine** System Changes)*

The teenage brain is wired to seek excitement, rewards, and social approval. This makes learning more effective when it's fun, personally meaningful, and gives quick feedback.

Adaptability and Growth (Brain Plasticity)

The adolescent brain is still flexible, making it a great time to build skills, form habits and shape identity. Encouraging a growth mindset – where mistakes are seen as part of learning – helps young people develop confidence and resilience.

What this means for learning:

- Make learning interactive and engaging – boring, passive lessons won't stick.
- Provide structure and support to help with planning and organisation.
- Connect learning to real life so it feels relevant and meaningful.
- Encourage healthy risks and self-reflection to build confidence and resilience.
- Use positive social influence – peer learning and mentoring can be powerful tools.

By understanding how the adolescent brain works, learning environments that support young people in becoming independent, motivated, and capable learners can be created.

Moment of Reflection 4.12: Practice

How can you encourage young people to explore creativity and risk taking to support their learning?

Mental Health and Resilience

Survival can often be misinterpreted as resilience or enterprise, but when you are working hard to keep your head above water the toll both mentally and physically is far higher than when hard work relates to ambition.

As learners develop, they learn the codes they will rely on throughout their lives. Their experiences and the response others have to those experiences shape them and these learned responses can be hard to unpick later in life if deemed to be unhealthy. For example, if as a learner you need to be responsible for others in your household, this responsibility will be a priority over study. Some learners carry more than just the burden of youth, and this can lead to limiting beliefs about their own ability and even future. It can also, however, develop ingenuity, creative thinking and tenacity.

A **scarcity mindset** (Mullainathan & Shafir, 2013) can develop from living in poverty and influence a person's decision making. For example, a scarcity mindset might encourage saving but not investing as this would be deemed too risky. If you live your life feeling like you might lose your wealth at any time, your outlook on the future will be different to someone who expects to earn/live a life of wealth. Similarly, if you are unhappy in your job but feel that you do not have enough time to commit to retraining or looking for another job, you might become stuck and work in a role which leads to burnout or be forced to leave rather than controlling the outcome. It is difficult to shift out of a scarcity mindset, particularly if you have believed it for a long time or it is compounded with other scarcity factors such as lack of money combined with perceived learning difficulties. Let's consider this scarcity mindset in relation to learners with additional learning needs. If you have been told or consider yourself to have a difficulty in a specific area of learning, for example reading, you might not envisage in your future becoming an author or even a practitioner. You will see that difficulty as something you need to avoid and will perhaps rely on other strengths or skills. This can lead to a focus on subjects which is too narrow and missing the variety of options when pursuing an interest as a career. It is almost a self-fulfilling prophecy where the skill which is considered a weakness is not practiced as much and therefore becomes much weaker than others.

Tunnel Vision and Short-Term Thinking

When you are in survival mode, it is difficult to plan long term and therefore when learners are used to living with a scarcity mindset, considering their future being beyond the next few weeks might be an impossibility for them. Exploring this with them in a non-threatening way will help them to envisage their future more broadly.

The Cycle of Scarcity and the Matthew Effect

The Matthew Effect was developed by Stanovich (1986) and explains how a learner living in a literacy rich environment will develop fluency and they will continue to improve their reading ability throughout their education. Those who find reading skills hard to master and do not seek out reading material or have the exposure to reading material in their home or school will fall behind their peers exponentially. Reading is a foundation of academic success so this gap will be evident in all subjects and will widen with time. In addition to this a learner's self-esteem drops as they realise the difference in their reading ability to their peers; this is a reinforcing feedback loop which is hard to break.

Moving from Passive to Active Engagement in the Classroom: The 'Where Will You Be in 5475 Days' Activity

One activity which would always elicit careful thought and a reframing of their current state was an activity which involved thinking about where you will be in 5475 days' time. This equates to 15 years, and for those of the learners who were 15–16 this put them beyond formal education and into the next stage of their life. They would likely have left home and may even have a family of their own by this time. In any case, they would no longer be dependent learners but adults. The next step is to consider what career they hoped to be doing at this point in their lives. This was sometimes not easy for the learners but once a single option was chosen, they would explore that they are doing right now which supported that vision. This was an eye-opening activity for most as they began to realise and connect the subjects they were currently studying to their future goals. They started to see how English, for example, in the case of the aspiring hockey coach, would give them the tools to communicate effectively, write match reports and even address the media. They began to see that mathematics gave them the skills to analyse and strategies on the pitch, using measures, graphs and equations to explain tactics to their team and plan their game strategy.

Sometimes when something feels hard you can become numb to it and go through the motions until it is complete. By connecting their current study to future aspirations, the purpose of their time at an education setting became clearer.

Dweck's (2006) research into **growth mindsets** resulted in several education settings adopting it as a way to support resilience and develop thinking skills. However, adopting an open mindset and hearing that hard work and persistence will get results can be difficult to hear for a learner that experiences challenges with learning every day and in spite of trying their hardest in every lesson, does not make the progress expected of them or that they see their peers achieve.

This chapter, whilst providing guidance on specific learning difficulties, has encouraged a reframing of this knowledge at regular intervals to support a strengths-based approach to meeting the needs of learners in the classroom; another important facet of an inclusive approach. When practitioners recognise and nurture these capabilities, within interconnected classrooms, learners flourish – not in spite of their differences but because of them.

Moments of Reflection

- 4.1 Interrelationships
- 4.2 Interrelationships
- 4.3 Practice
- 4.4 Multiple Perspectives
- 4.5 Practice
- 4.6 Curiosity
- 4.7 Interrelationships
- 4.8 Curiosity
- 4.9 Practice
- 4.10 Curiosity
- 4.11 Multiple Perspectives
- 4.12 Practice

References

American Psychiatric Association. (2013). *Diagnostic and statistical manual of mental disorders: DSM-5* (5th ed.). American Psychiatric Publishing. https://psychiatryonline.org/doi/book/10.1176/appi.books.9780890425596

Barber, I. (2024, December 18). The Delphi study: Implications of a new definition of dyslexia. https://dyslexiaaction.org.uk/2024/12/the-delphi-study-a-new-definition-of-dyslexia/#:~:text=What%20is%20the%20new%20Delphi,to%20the%20impact%20of%20dyslexia.%E2%80%9D

Blank, R., Barnett, A. L., Cairney, J., Green, D., Kirby, A., Polatjko, H. et al. (2019). International clinical practice recommendations on the definition, diagnosis, intervention, and psychosocial aspects of developmental coordination disorder. *Developmental Medicine and Child Neurology, 61*(3), 242–285.

British Dyslexia Association. (2018). What is dyslexia? www.bdadyslexia.org.uk/dyslexia/what-is-dyslexia

Bronfenbrenner, U. (1979). *The ecology of human development: Experiments by nature and design*. Harvard University Press. www.simplypsychology.org/bronfenbrenner.html

Carroll, J., Holden, C., Kirby, P., Thompson, P. A., & Snowling, M. J. (2025). Toward a consensus on dyslexia: Findings from a Delphi study. *Journal of Child Psychology and Psychiatry, 66*(7), 1065–1076.

Dweck, C. S. (2006). *Mindset: The new psychology of success*. Random House.

Elliott, J. G., & Grigorenko, E. L. (2014). *The dyslexia debate*. Cambridge University Press.

International Dyslexia Association. (2002) Definition of dyslexia. https://dyslexiaida.org/definition-of-dyslexia

Li, H., Cui, B., & Sun, Y. (2024). The prevalence of developmental coordination disorder in children: A systematic review and metanalysis. *Frontiers in Paediatrics, 12,* 1387406.

Milton, D. (2012). On the ontological status of autism: The 'double empathy problem'. *Disability & Society, 27*(6), 883–887. https://doi.org/10.1080/09687599.2012.710008

Mullainathan, S., & Shafir, E. (2013). *Scarcity: Why having too little means so much*. Times Books.

Murray, D., Lesser, M., & Lawson, W. (1995). Attention, monotropism and the diagnostic criteria for autism. *Autism: The International Journal of Research and Practice, 1*(2), 117–132.

NICE. (n.d.). NICE guidance. www.nice.org.uk/guidance

Rose, J. (2009). *Identifying and teaching children and young people with dyslexia and literacy difficulties*. Department for Children, Schools & Families. www.thedyslexia-spldtrust.org.uk/media/downloads/inline/the-rose-report.1294933674.pdf

SpLD Assessment Standards Committee (SASC). (n.d.). Maths difficulties and dyscalculia guidance. www.sasc.org.uk

Stanovich, K. E. (1986). Matthew effects in reading: Some consequences of individual differences in the acquisition of literacy. *Reading Research Quarterly, 21*(4), 360–407.

5
The Process of Learning

Overview

This chapter builds on the specific learning difficulty analysis carried out in Chapter 4 and draws the focus to key cognitive skills, which when addressed in the classroom can make a noticeable impact for learners who are finding learning challenging. It was necessary to explore the labels which are most likely to be assigned to learners in the classroom, but at the same time, consider skills essential for learning and their role in learning differences. Whether these differences are lifelong such as dyslexia or temporary like anxiety or stress the impact they have on learning is the same.

As discussed earlier in Chapter 3, the advantage of a transdiagnostic approach is that it limits the possibility of individuals being pigeonholed which subsequently limits both expectations and support for that learner.

To begin this chapter is a letter from Lara Furmidge, an experienced primary headteacher who now mentors prospective headteachers. She applied several strategies from cognitive science when she was in her leadership role and continues to support schools in addressing challenges through targeted, evidence-based approaches.

DOI: 10.4324/9781003400639-6

Moment of Reflection 5.1: Interrelationships

As you read Lara's letter, consider the following: if you are unfamiliar with **Rosenshine's principles**, spend some time reading through them here: www.teachertoolkit.co.uk/wp-content/uploads/2018/10/Principles-of-Insruction-Rosenshine.pdf

Dear practitioner,

Pedagogy and SEND

Pedagogy is defined as 'The art, science or profession of teaching children' (Merriam-Webster, n.d.).

In most schools this has been the conversation for the last few years – schools are considering what their 'quality first teaching', their pedagogical approach looks like. How can this development improve outcomes for all learners?

We also have a great deal of research at our fingertips – this now winds through all stages of learning as a practitioner – Initial Teacher Training (ITT) to National Professional Qualification for Leading (NPQL). We have more than we have ever had before; easily accessible to all – not buried in a huge volume of academic language.

Rosenshine's (2012) Principles of Instruction

Schools thinking about how these tools are used and the precision of the use is so important. Modelling has been discussed in schools for the length of time I have been in education, but it has not always been effective; it has not always shown learners the thought process that goes behind the activity we are doing – the thoughts going through my head as I write this.

There is a great deal of support out there for schools in the development of these tools – I began with Teaching WalkThroughs: Five Step Guides to Instructional Coaching by Tom Sherrington and Oliver Caviglioli (2020). The theory was easy to share with staff to secure the 'why' and buy-in. As a school (like many others) we took our time to look at our pedagogy and implement our tools well.

Education Endowment Foundation (2025) guidance states: 'Pupils with Special Educational Needs and Disability (SEND) have the greatest need for excellent teaching and are entitled to provision that supports achievement at, and enjoyment of, school'.

The attainment gap between pupils with SEND and their peers is twice as big as the gap between pupils eligible for free school meals and their peers.

Below are there five evidence-based recommendations to support pupils with SEND.

1. *Create a positive and supportive environment for all pupils, without exception.*
2. *Build an ongoing, holistic understanding of your pupils and their needs.*
3. *Ensure all pupils have access to high-quality teaching.*
4. *Complement high-quality teaching with carefully selected small-group and one-to-one interventions.*
5. *Work effectively with teaching assistants.*

The right focus on ***high-quality teaching*** *is point 3. This is then broken down into:*

- *To a great extent, good teaching for pupils with SEND is good teaching for all.*
- *Searching for a 'magic bullet' can distract teachers from the powerful strategies they often already possess.*
- *The research suggests a group of teaching strategies that teachers should consider emphasising for pupils with SEND. Teachers should develop a repertoire of these strategies.*

They can be used flexibly in response to the needs of all pupils:

- *Flexible grouping*
- *Cognitive and metacognitive strategies*
- *Explicit instruction*
- *Using technology to support pupils with SEND*
- *Scaffolding*

And point one is key – this is high-quality teaching for all – so done well it will accelerate learning.

Section 6.37 of the Code of Practice (Department of Education & Department of Health and Social Care, 2014) states ***'High quality teaching, differentiated for individual pupils, is the first step in responding to pupils who have or may have SEN'.***

This is the legislative guidance that all schools must abide by.

However, even with all this guidance, research, school knowing (and doing) to develop the tools of their pedagogy – review, small steps for new material, questioning, checking for understanding, modelling, scaffolding, guided practice, independent practice . . . – outcomes for SEND are still a major issue.

Reading educational press, following practitioners on social media, talking to friends both in mainstream and SEND experts – SEND progress is a real hot topic – the outcomes are not there.

I am also a SEND parent as well as an ex Primary Headteacher. The research and pedagogy tool development are an area I passionately believe will raise standards, developing learners who will be prepared for the future (the curriculum is a whole different discussion). However, having seen my child move through the stages of education there is a vital area missing.

As a Primary Headteacher I know my EYFS teachers (in a nutshell) need a thorough knowledge of letters – sound correspondence, phonemic awareness, systematic phonics progression and teaching strategies. It is detailed knowledge and practice that combined with 'high-quality teaching' and pedagogy gives learners the best start to reading. We know what the learners need to be taught to be good readers.

My child is a 'K' learner – diagnosis of dyslexia and dyscalculia. At every stage of her educational life, the knowledge of these areas of need is not there. The high-quality teaching and pedagogy were either in place or developing but the knowledge of 'the what' and 'the how' (the systematic phonics progression with the phonics analogy) is not there.

Dyslexia knowledge is better (not great) and dyscalculia basically non-existent. Every time we start a new phase; we have the same conversation about the how and the what. Quite simply they don't know how to teach the area of need. The Code of Practice gives us four broad areas of need; we can have all or some at any time. Do we have all of the basics we need to teach? If you have a child with a diagnosis of autism in your class – do you have the 'phonemic awareness' to teach them? If you have a dyscalculic learner do you have the basic understanding of how this can impact on a learner and how to teach them (pedagogy)?

So yes, we need high-quality teaching based on researched pedagogy – we need to know to use the right tools for the job. We need to be inclusive – know the strengths of every learner and build on these – relationships. But we need to be trained in the basics of all four areas of needs – properly: for all teachers, in all phases and all subjects.

Being a SEND parent did make me a better Head (a whole other conversation) but I am teaching myself the knowledge. As a parent I need to stop having the same conversation with SENDCos, teachers, headteachers about the basic knowledge – but if they have not had basic training then I can't.

Lara Furmidge

Moment of Reflection 5.2: Multiple Perspectives

Lara's letter is in two parts; the first relates to pedagogy and strategies for the classroom; consider her top five and which you are currently implementing and which you might like to try in your setting.

Now reflect upon her perspective as a parent. Take time to reflect upon your initial reactions to her experience and consider all players in the situation. How could her daughter's experience of education have been improved?

It can be common for strategies to be recommended in isolation. For example, a learner with dyslexia might be recommended to chunk information in order to remember it and the same advice may be given for a learner with ADHD to reduce the time needed to focus on the information. Same advice but different intentions. These could each be recommended separately and not combined.

Suggested in Figure 5.1 is a learning system which interrelates the different theories of learning around the central idea of working memory. This will be the central 'node' in the learning system.

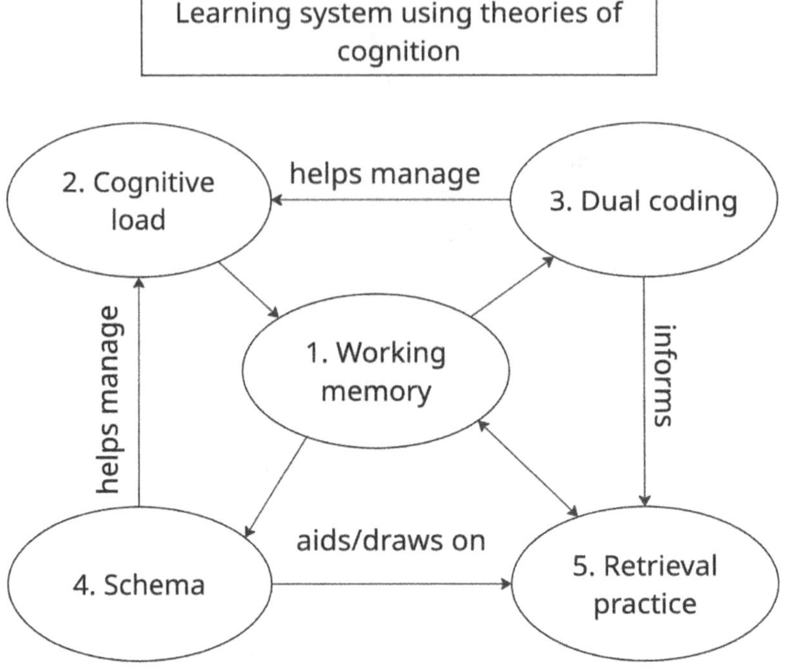

Figure 5.1 A diagram to outline the connections between popular cognitive theories related to attention and retention

1. Working Memory

Theories of working memory have been highlighted particularly in relation to cognitive load because of its synthesis of known and unknown information, and the most referred to and cited theory of working memory is Baddeley and Hitch's model from 1974.

This working memory model model states that working memory is a limited-capacity system that is responsible for holding and processing information temporarily.

The model consists of four main components:

- The **central executive:** This is the supervisory system that controls the other two components. It is responsible for allocating attention, switching between tasks, and suppressing irrelevant information.
- The **phonological loop:** This is a verbal-based system that is responsible for storing and processing auditory information. It consists of two parts:

a phonological store, which holds auditory information for a short period of time, and an articulatory rehearsal process, which allows the information to be refreshed by subvocal rehearsal.
- The **visuospatial sketchpad:** This is a system that is responsible for storing and processing visual and spatial information. It is thought to be made up of two components: a visual cache, which holds visual information for a short period of time, and a spatial sketchpad, which allows the information to be manipulated and transformed.
- **Episodic buffer** (Baddeley 2000): This later addition was added to integrate information – visual, audio and from the long-term memory. It combines to create 'episodes'.

Baddeley and Hitch's working memory model has been influential and remained popular since its inception, and whilst there are other models of memory, it is working memory which has caught the attention of education professionals and has been identified as a key area for strategies and recommendations relating to focus, memory, retention and recall.

Some of the limitations of the working memory model:

- The model does not fully explain how information is transferred from working memory to long-term memory. The connection between the temporary holding store of information and how it subsequently turns into a memory leaves practitioners with unanswered questions of how to make information memorable. The working memory model might have informed us that the brain's capacity to store new information is fairly limited, but not how it stores information or how it assimilates known information.
- The model does not account for the role of emotions in working memory.
- The model does not account for the role of attention in working memory, so whilst the central executive might assign attention, how it is captured in the first place is not explained.

How this relates to literacy difficulties or challenges with processing verbally presented information might sound complicated but it isn't when you break it down. If the processing difficulties that learners with dyslexia have are considered, it can be seen that one component is called the phonological loop. It is known that learners with dyslexia find processing sounds in words a challenge, therefore it's logical to draw the assumption that they are going to find verbally presented information more difficult to process. They are not going to make use of the processing capacity of the phonological loop.

Figure 5.2 shows the working memory with the traits of learning differences mapped to it, taking into consideration attention, code switching, auditory processing and retrieval.

Moment of Reflection 5.3: Interrelationships

What if we thought about memory as a story rather than a store. How could we make information more memorable and impactful if we played with how it was presented?

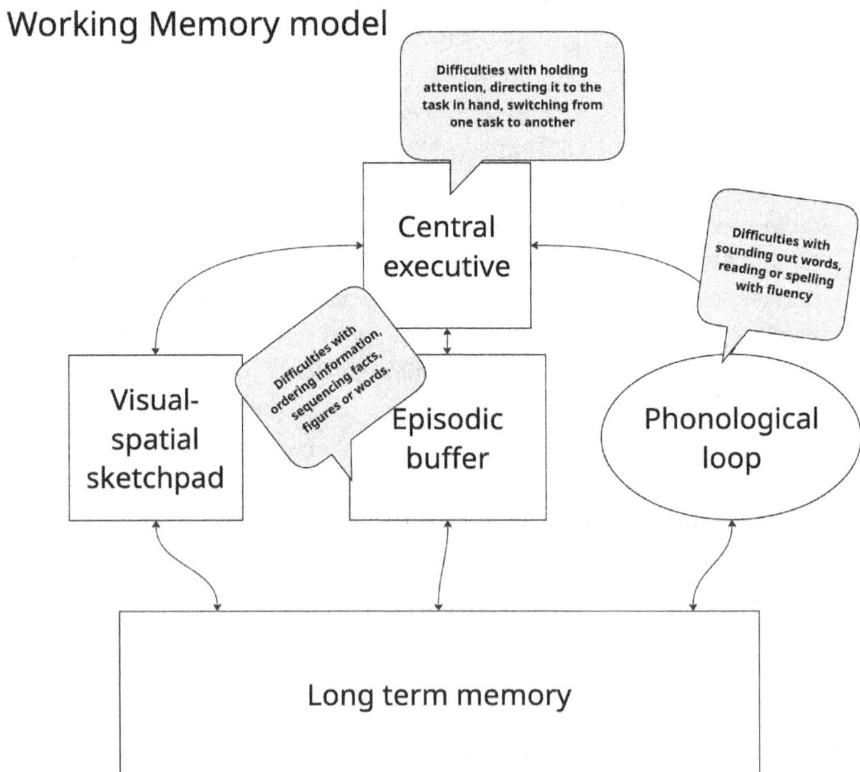

Figure 5.2 Working memory and specific learning difficulties

2. Cognitive Load: A Popular Strategy

This next theory has led to recommendations for classroom practices such as interleaving, spaced practice and knowledge organisers. It is referenced in Ofsted and the Education Endowment Foundation (2018); their research into metacognition and self-regulation, which features managing cognitive load, has one of the highest ratings of performance for cost and efficacy.

Cognitive load is the theory by Sweller (1988) and its definition is the total amount of information that you are processing at any one time. This load is split between **intrinsic and extrinsic loads**. Intrinsic being the information which is presented, so your content, and extrinsic being the variables which are outside of that content. An example of extrinsic load is background noise, choice of font or presentation of information.

Figure 5.3 An image of a classroom

Moment of Reflection 5.4: Curiosity

Consider the **extraneous variables** that might exist in a typical classroom. Consider sound, light, position of both the practitioner and the learners and your choices as a practitioner regarding how information is shared.

Addressing the extraneous can be achieved through:

- reducing classroom distractions to ensure that rooms are quiet
- keeping conversation to a minimum in order for the intrinsic load to be the main area of focus
- ensuring classroom displays are carefully considered for appearance and content.

Moment of Reflection 5.5: Multiple Perspectives

Track the attention capacity of one of your classes or a group of learners. What is the range of the length of time individuals can focus for? How might this affect your planning?

What would be their response if you asked them how long they think they can focus for before it becomes uncomfortable?

For a learner with **sensory integration difficulties**, this control of the extrinsic environment can be advantageous because they find it difficult to filter out that extra noise and for learners with dyslexia reducing the amount of information and providing summaries to ensure that the key points are being understood will always make classroom practice easier.

In addition to this, disadvantage takes up more brain space and subsequently cognitive load. When you're hungry or tired or worried about your family situation, your capacity to learn is diminished. Everyone can sometimes find it difficult to focus, especially with some subjects or life events that threaten to monopolise the mental load available to function. Learners may not yet have the maturity or strategies in order to cope with the demands on their attention successfully.

However, what Sweller's theory, if it is applied without reflection, misses is the nuance. Several learners benefit from speaking their ideas before recording them. They enjoy thinking out loud and organising their thoughts through discussion and being given the opportunity to sound out these ideas and gain validation that they are on the right track. Removing the opportunity for whole class discussion can mean many learners are left relying on their secretarial skills.

The advantages of understanding learning as a neurological process is that teaching activities and planning can ensure that the information shared has the most potential to be recalled. However, if the approach taken is from a neurotypical perspective, and it is already known that the neurological pathways for individuals with ADHD, autism and dyslexia are not typical, there is the potential to overlook their needs.

It is pertinent to stress that being mindful of the cognitive load of information is important but this has to be considered in the context of individual needs, and this approach alone is not sufficient. It is also imperative that consideration is taken in regards to the perception of the cognitive load. If you are focused on the content and not the delivery for example, you may overlook the load of the language you are using or the novelty of the information for the learners.

Cognitive Load Checklist

✓ Extraneous load: Environment, worksheets, seating plans
✓ Language load: Vocabulary choice, subject-specific terminology
✓ Content load: Amount to learn, time to repeat, complexity, novelty

3. Dual Coding Theory

Dual coding is a theory of cognition that suggests that the mind processes information along two different channels; verbal and visual. It was hypothesised by Allan Paivio of the University of Western Ontario in 1971. In developing this theory, Paivio used the idea that the formation of mental images aids learning through the picture superiority effect.

This directly relates to working memory which makes use of visual spatial sketchpad and phonological loop. The main benefit to this approach is that information can also be visually presented for those who find it difficult to follow verbal instructions. And those with difficulties with processing visual information have the verbal instructions.

The verbal system is responsible for processing information that is presented in words, while the visual system is responsible for processing information that is presented in images. These two systems are thought to be separate and independent, but they are also thought to be interconnected.

The benefit of this theory is that it can be applied to designing effective learning material and to help learners to better understand new concepts. It can manage some of the novelty cognitive load by providing an accessible introduction to a topic.

Here are some tips for using dual coding in education:

- Use a variety of visual aids, such as diagrams, pictures and graphs, but make sure the picture used does not add to the cognitive load or distract from the main point.
- Use clear and concise language.
- Avoid overloading the learner with too much information at once.
- Provide opportunities for the learner to practice what they have learned.
- Give the learner feedback on their performance.

This theory proposes that information is encoded in both verbal and non-verbal systems, creating interconnected memory traces. Visualising an apple activates both its name and sensory details, potentially enhancing recall.

This theory lends itself well to multisensory teaching which is often recommended for learners with specific learning difficulties. There is further information, including free resources for the classroom, on this website: www.olicav.com.

Visualising can be challenging for many learners, especially those who are learning the foundations of language; there is a focus on phonics in early years which is evidence based and best practice. However, being able to create pictures can support the acquisition of new vocabulary and also aids recall.

Moment of Reflection 5.6: Practice

Using one of the models mentioned above, plan an activity which would maximise the potential for retention and recall.

How much of what you already do takes this model into account? What do you need to do differently?

Have you considered your own capacity for information?

What is your method of retaining information and is it something which would be useful to share with your cohort?

4. Schema

Building on dual coding is the theory of schema. Schema is a mental model of connected ideas or concepts stored in long-term memory (Nickerson, 2024). It is a framework that can be used to organise and interpret new information. Schemas can be specific, such as a schema for a dog, or they can be more general, such as a schema for animals.

We use schemas all the time without even realising it. When a person sees a dog, for example, the schema for dogs is automatically activated. This schema dictates what to expect, such as that dogs have four legs, fur and a tail. It is based on previously held knowledge and can become more detailed as the person learns more about the subject.

The crucial question is, how can this building of schemas be supported? Working memory capacity cannot be improved but how it is used can be influenced. At the very least, a practitioner can be mindful about the information shared.

Here are some ways to apply schema theory in the classroom:

- **Activate learners' prior knowledge.** Before teaching a new concept, activate learners' prior knowledge by asking them questions about what they already know about the topic. This will help them to connect the new information to what they already know, which will make it easier for them to learn.
- **Use visuals and graphic organisers.** Visuals and graphic organisers can help learners to visualise and organise new information. This can make it easier for them to understand and remember the information.
- **Provide opportunities for hands-on learning.** Hands-on learning helps learners to make connections between the new information and their own experiences. This can help them to better understand and remember the information.
- **Use scaffolding.** Scaffolding is the process of providing support to learners as they learn new information. This can be done by providing them with hints, cues and questions.
- **Teach learners how to use schemas.** Help learners to understand how schemas work and how they can use them to learn new information. This can be done by explicitly teaching them about schemas and by giving them opportunities to practice using them.

By applying schema theory in the classroom, teachers can help learners to learn new information more easily and effectively.

Moment of Reflection 5.7: Interrelationships

How can you categorise the information you share and strengthen the schemas which your learners are building?

5. Retrieval Practice

Retrieval practice is a learning strategy that involves studying information over multiple intervals of time, rather than all at once. This helps to consolidate the information in long-term memory and make it more resistant to forgetting. It also supports the working memory as it encourages little and often rather than lots of information all in one go.

There are many ways to implement spaced retrieval in education. One common approach is to use flashcards. Learners can be given a set of flashcards to study, and then be quizzed on them at regular intervals. The intervals can be gradually increased over time, as the learners become more familiar with the material.

Another approach is to use practice tests. Learners can be given practice tests on the material they are learning, and then receive feedback on their performance. This helps them to identify areas where they need more practice. Spaced retrieval can be used to improve learning in a variety of subjects, including math, science, history and language arts. It is a particularly effective strategy for learning factual information, such as vocabulary words, historical dates and mathematical formulas.

Here are some of the benefits of using spaced retrieval in education:

- It can help to improve long-term retention of information.
- It can make information more resistant to forgetting.
- It can help learners to identify areas where they need more practice.
- It can help learners to develop a deeper understanding of the material.
- It can be motivating and engaging for learners.

A limitation of applying retrieval strategies without considering the learner as a whole is that they can be restrictive and fixed. Ensure that any strategy can be adapted, reviewed and changed depending on feedback from the learners.

One school I worked with introduced knowledge maps and these became integral to homework. The use of knowledge maps was not as widespread as the school had hoped, and we soon realised that they weren't being referred to by the learners when they were completing their homework. This disappointed the senior leadership team who had spent a lot of time and effort in developing them. It was only through a focus group working with learners that the senior leadership team found out that the majority of the students accessed this document on their phones and it was too small to refer to; it therefore was an underused resource. We then made printed copies available and the students used them more often to support homework.

Moment of Reflection 5.8: Interrelationships

As you read this case study consider mapping out the times when Charlie might need additional support. What might that look like and how can it inform their revision and consolidation when they are at home?

Case Study 2: A 17-Year-Old Learner with Processing Difficulties Falling Behind in Science

Background: Charlie, a 17-year-old secondary school learner preparing for their A-levels.

Primary Challenge: Charlie has cognitive processing difficulties, particularly in processing and retaining information, which impacts their ability to keep up with the demands of their science subjects (Biology, Chemistry and Physics).

Impact: Charlie has fallen behind in their science coursework, struggles to keep pace with lessons and finds it difficult to complete assignments and revise effectively for exams.

Key Challenges

Processing Speed and Retention Issues:

- Difficulty with Complex Concepts: Charlie struggles to process and understand complex scientific theories and equations at the same speed as their peers. This does not mean they are incapable but it takes them longer.
- Slow Information Retention: They find it difficult to retain new information from lessons, often needing more time to absorb and understand scientific terms, formulas and concepts.
- Trouble with Multistep Tasks: Charlie has difficulty following and completing multistep experiments or calculations, leading to confusion, incomplete work and lots of stress for them.

Falling Behind in Coursework:

- Missed Deadlines: Due to their processing difficulties, Charlie takes longer to complete assignments and frequently misses submission deadlines, which has resulted in lower grades. They will speak with their class practitioner but often have more than one deadline from their other subjects which creates a backlog for them that is sometimes difficult to manage.
- Class Participation: In-class tasks, especially those involving group discussions or quick responses, are challenging for Charlie, and they often feel left behind. They do well when given the time to respond but in hands-up tasks, they struggle to participate.
- Struggles with Independent Revision: Charlie has difficulty managing their time effectively during revision periods and becomes overwhelmed by the volume of content they need to revise, which has negatively affected their exam preparation.

Low Confidence and Motivation:

- Decreased Self-Esteem: As Charlie has fallen behind in science, their confidence has declined, and they have become increasingly anxious about their academic performance. They really enjoy science as a subject and are hoping to continue to study it at university but are beginning to doubt themselves.

- Avoidance Behaviour: Due to their struggles, Charlie has started avoiding science revision and lab work, feeling that they cannot keep up with the class, further contributing to them falling behind.

Systems Thinking Approach to Support

Identifying Key Leverage Points:

- Time Management and Organisation: Charlie requires structured strategies to manage their time effectively and break down tasks into manageable parts.
- Individualised Support: Tailoring lessons and tasks to accommodate their processing difficulties, providing more time for them to absorb information and complete assignments.
- Confidence Building: Creating opportunities for Charlie to rebuild their confidence by celebrating small successes and encouraging participation in less time-pressured environments.

Developing Intervention Strategies:

- Breaking Down Tasks: Teachers and support staff break down complex scientific topics into smaller, more digestible sections, allowing Charlie to focus on one concept at a time without becoming overwhelmed.

Extra Time and Scaffolding:

- Providing extended time for assignments and exams to allow Charlie to process information at their own pace.
- Offering step-by-step guidance in experiments and problem-solving activities, ensuring that Charlie can follow multistep processes without losing track.

Use of Technology:

- Introducing assistive technology (e.g., speech-to-text software, digital organisers) to help Charlie organise their thoughts, complete written assignments more efficiently, and record lessons for later review.

In-Class Support and Accommodations

Classroom Support:

- A teaching assistant (TA) is assigned to provide additional in-class support, helping Charlie with note-taking, organising their work, and following along with group tasks.
- Teachers provide key summaries and simplified notes for each topic to help Charlie focus on core concepts without being overwhelmed by excessive detail.
- Differentiated Instruction: Teachers adapt lesson delivery for Charlie by using more visual aids, such as diagrams, flowcharts and videos, to help them process information more effectively.

Structured Revision and Study Strategies:

- Revision Plans: A tailored revision plan is created for Charlie, breaking their science subjects into smaller, manageable chunks of content, allowing for spaced repetition and review over time.
- Study Aids: Flashcards, mind maps, and other visual tools are introduced to help Charlie recall key terms and concepts more easily.

Confidence and Motivation Support:

- Building Success: Teachers set achievable, short-term goals for Charlie, such as completing a portion of a project or mastering a particular concept, to help them experience success and rebuild their self-esteem.
- Positive Reinforcement: Charlie receives positive feedback and encouragement for their efforts, even in small tasks, to keep them motivated and reduce feelings of failure or anxiety.
- Peer Support: Pairing Charlie with a supportive peer for group work to encourage collaboration and foster a positive learning environment.

Implementation and Support

Collaborating with Parents:

- Home Support Plan: Teachers and parents work together to implement a home study schedule that reflects the support Charlie receives in school, reinforcing their time management and revision strategies.
- Regular Communication: Teachers provide regular updates to Charlie's parents about their progress and any adjustments needed in their support plan.

School-Based Support:

- SENCo Involvement: The Special Educational Needs Coordinator (SENCo) creates an individualised education plan for Charlie, outlining specific accommodations and interventions based on their processing difficulties.
- Weekly Check-Ins: Charlie has regular meetings with a learning mentor or TA to discuss their progress, address any concerns, and adjust support as needed.

Exam Accommodations:

- Extra Time: Charlie is tested for additional time in exams to accommodate their slower processing speed.
- Use of Technology: Access to a computer for typing or using speech-to-text software during exams to help them complete written tasks more efficiently.

Outcomes

Improved Academic Progress:

- With structured support, Charlie begins catching up in their science subjects. Their teachers notice improvements in their ability to follow and complete assignments, particularly when given additional time and clearer, step-by-step instructions.
- Charlie's exam performance improves, as the extra time allows them to process and recall information without feeling rushed.

Enhanced Study Skills:

- Charlie learns and adopts new study techniques, such as breaking down content into manageable parts and using visual tools like mind maps. These strategies help them retain information more effectively and manage their workload.
- Their use of assistive technology improves their ability to organise their notes and complete assignments more independently.

Increased Confidence and Engagement:

- As Charlie experiences academic success, their confidence grows. They are more willing to participate in class discussions and group work, knowing they have the tools and support to keep up with their peers.
- Their motivation to study increases as they begin to feel more in control of their learning and see tangible improvements in their science subjects.

Reduced Anxiety:

- With a structured support system in place, Charlie experiences less anxiety about falling behind in science. The combination of one-on-one tutoring, extra time, and differentiated tasks helps them feel less overwhelmed by the coursework.
- As their academic performance improves, Charlie's overall outlook on school and learning becomes more positive, reducing their avoidance behaviour.

The Value of Centring Working Memory and Its Relation to Specific Learning Difficulties

Applying an understanding of working memory to your teaching has several advantages:

1. Working memory plays a role in several learning difficulties.
2. It provides an understanding of why people learn at different rates.
3. Being mindful of working memory, especially at the beginning of a new topic or one with lots of complex, new information can support the successful retention of that information (Alloway & Alloway, 2014).

Sensory Interruptions to Focus

Challenges to a person's capacity for information happen all the time. For example, have you ever turned the radio down when driving as it has become busy with traffic, or you're in an unfamiliar area? Maybe that's just me. Some learners may find it difficult to switch their focus from something which has happened recently to a classroom activity and therefore their capacity to take on new information can be compromised. This might be as a result of an event which they have been unable to forget or 'park' in order to focus, or it might be intrusive thoughts that are impossible to ignore. It will be difficult to shift this learner's thinking to the task in hand without acknowledging their issue.

Moment of Reflection 5.9: Interrelationships

What is your current strategy to deal with those queries at the beginning of a lesson?

Code Switching

Before you begin to teach new information you want to ensure the learner is ready to learn and this can often mean cueing them in with subject-specific language and expectation. This is related to a concept known as code switching, and being explicit with the expectations of a subject will support a young person's preparation for that subject.

Each school subject has its own linguistic code, including:

- Vocabulary: Specialised words with precise meanings.
- Syntax and Structure: Different ways of constructing explanations and arguments.
- Ways of Thinking: Unique modes of reasoning and problem solving.

Examples of Code-Switching Between Subjects

1. Mathematics → English Literature

Learners switching from mathematics to English must shift from a concise, formulaic way of thinking to one that is interpretive and expressive.

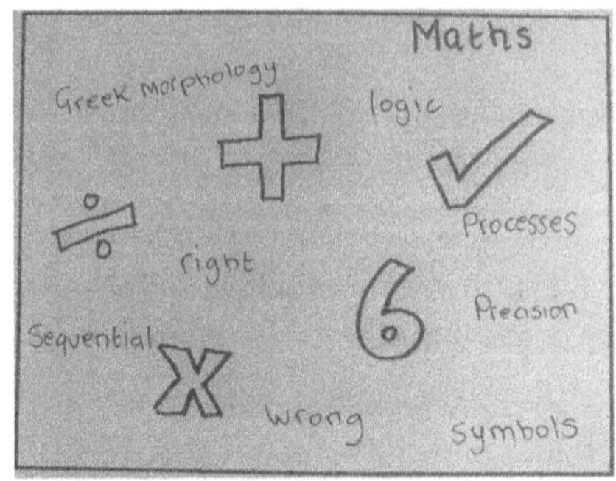

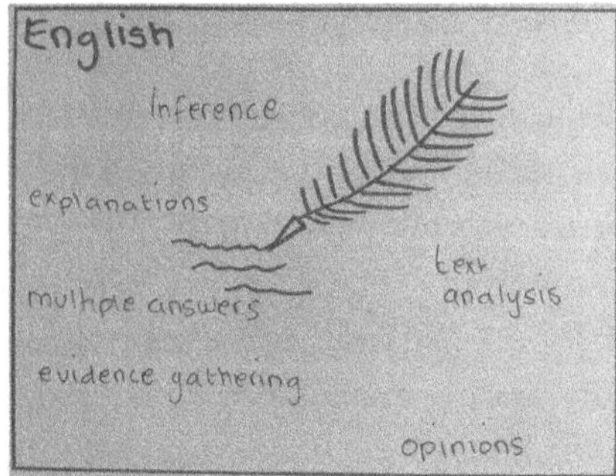

Figure 5.4 Maths vs. English

Mathematics Code: Precise, symbolic, rule-driven. Example: 'The equation $2x + 3 = 9$ simplifies to $x = 3$'.

English Literature Code: Descriptive, analytical, open to multiple interpretations. Example: 'The author uses imagery to convey a sense of nostalgia and longing'.

Challenge: A learner moving from solving equations to writing an essay may struggle with the sudden need for extended prose rather than direct, numerical answers.

2. Science → History

Science requires logical reasoning, technical vocabulary, and empirical evidence, whereas history involves narrative thinking, argumentation, and evaluating sources.

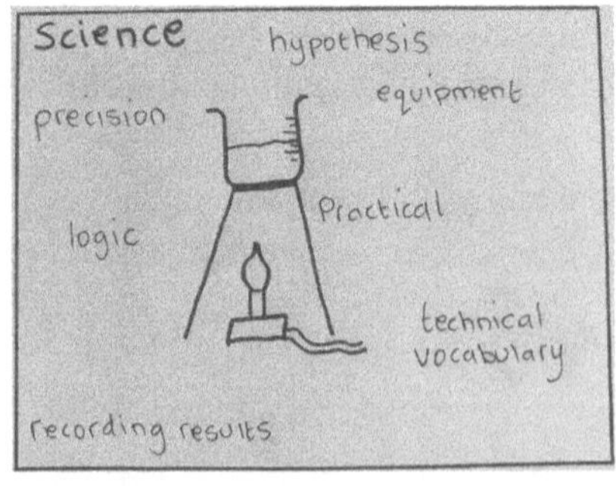

Figure 5.5 Science vs. history

Science Code: Objective, based on experimentation and hypothesis testing. Example: 'The chemical reaction between hydrogen and oxygen produces water'.

History Code: Analytical, requires weighing perspectives and context. Example: 'The causes of the French Revolution were influenced by economic hardship and political unrest'.

Challenge: A learner leaving a structured science lab to engage in a historical debate must shift from focusing on empirical certainty to considering multiple interpretations of past events.

3. Art → Science

Art encourages creativity, subjective interpretation and free expression, whereas science requires precision, classification and factual accuracy.

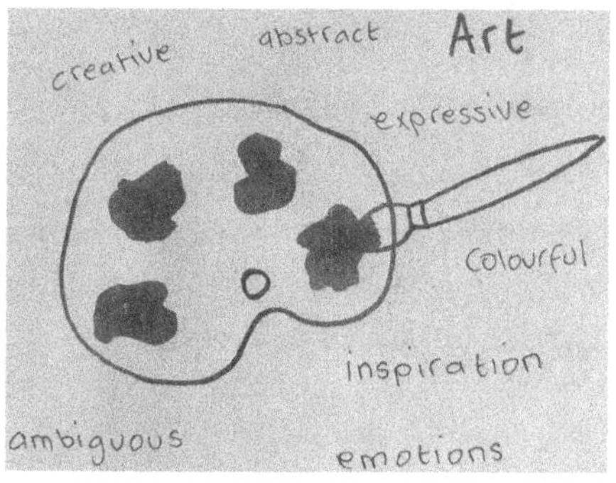

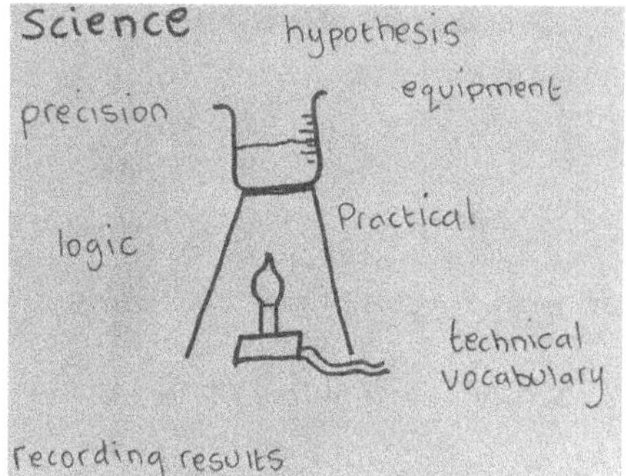

Figure 5.6 Art vs. science

Art Code: Emphasises aesthetics, emotion and personal expression. Example: 'The bold use of colour in this painting conveys a sense of movement and energy'.

Science Code: Emphasises logic, structured methodology and objectivity. Example: 'Cells are classified into eukaryotic and prokaryotic based on their structural differences'.

Challenge: A learner moving from an art class (where ideas are subjective and open-ended) to a science lesson (where accuracy and classification matter) must shift their cognitive approach significantly.

Switching between these academic codes places a cognitive demand on learners:

- Working Memory Strain: Retaining subject-specific terminology and mental frameworks.
- Mental Fatigue: The frequent transitions between different styles of thinking.
- Processing Speed: Some learners may need extra time to adjust to a new subject's linguistic and conceptual demands.

Learners who struggle with executive function (such as those with dyslexia or ADHD) may find these transitions especially challenging.

Moment of Reflection 5.10: Interrelationships

Over the course of the week, record how long it takes a class to settle and what their previous lesson was. Reflect on what might make the transition more challenging and what you can do to support them to tune into their current subject.

How to Support Code Switching

Explicitly Teach Subject-Specific Codes

- Introduce key vocabulary before starting a lesson.
- Model how to transition between different styles of thinking.

Use Bridging Strategies Between Subjects

- Encourage connections between disciplines (e.g., using storytelling in science to explain discoveries).
- Compare and contrast how reasoning works across subjects.

Give Learners Time to Transition

- Use short activities or discussions to help learners shift from one subject's code to another.
- Encourage metacognition (e.g., 'How is explaining a concept in science different from writing an argument in history?').

Encourage Multimodal Learning

- Use diagrams, hands-on activities, and discussions to support different modes of thinking.
- Allow learners to express concepts in multiple ways (e.g., explaining a math concept verbally before solving it algebraically).

How to manage a learner with limited working memory capacity is a bit more challenging as it involves considering your planning, delivery and the content. Whilst a practitioner's perspective might change on how labels are assigned for certain challenges in the classroom, those challenges will remain and can be significant for lots of learners, both with and without a diagnosis. Working memory is closely related to processing and plays a crucial role in the ability to attend to, take in and respond to information. It is also a key factor in the learning difficulties below.

Why the Way Processing Information Is Important But Not in a Left Brain, Right Brain Kind of Way

There are studies into processing which have identified a neurotypical route for words and language both spoken or written (Galaburda & Sanides, 1980). This information is then stored as long-term memory and subsequently retrieved. This is the most efficient way of processing written language. A person with dyslexia may attempt to process the information using visual cues, and MRI scans have shown that the areas of the brain that are active in a dyslexic brain are different to those of a non-dyslexic brain. This inevitably leads to a less efficient processing of this information and is likely to take the dyslexic person longer. Especially if the information being processed is written language without any visual aids.

Furthermore, if you have a reading difficulty and you find it difficult to recognise words, then some of your processing capacity will be shifted to deal with breaking down and understanding of those words. If your reading difficulty is significant, then you may have to isolate each letter to process, then put them together as a word. Again more of the processing capacity is being redirected from the task.

Let's add another layer in here, say you have a limited vocabulary as well as a reading difficulty. Not only are you trying to understand the words on either a letter or a word level, but you are also now trying to comprehend the words themselves. Again, more processing ability is being taken up by that task. It is evident that someone who experiences challenges with learning can experience interruptions from their neurodivergent needs, emotions or basic needs, and how frustrating it must be having to commit so much processing capacity to tasks which others in the class can do automatically.

The Neurotypical Capacity for Instructions

In a standard classroom, it is likely there will be learners with processing capacities across the range of these averages making meeting all their needs a challenge for teachers.

- 5–6 years: 2 instructions
- 7–9 years: 3 instructions
- 10–12 years: 4 instructions
- 13–15 years: 5 instructions
- 16–29 years: 6 instructions (Alloway & Alloway, 2014)

Moment of Reflection 5.11: Curiosity

Consider the models and strategies outlined in this chapter and use a traffic light system (Red: wouldn't work; Amber: might give it a go; Green: would definitely work).

Consider each one in relation to your cohort and as individuals.

Finally reflect upon it as part of your VSM and what it would need in regard to communication (system 2) and planning (systems 3). How would it be received by the setting in general? (systems 4 and 5).

A lot has been covered in this chapter and systems thinking has supported interrelating cognitive theories into a learning system which can flex to the needs of your learners. What matters is how these theories are applied thoughtfully and without too many assumptions. One day it might be important to reduce distractions in the classroom whilst another day it is relying on visual prompts and talking partners. It is not about finding the right strategies but noticing what a learner of the cohort needs right now and being flexible enough to adapt.

Whether a practitioner is planning a lesson, supporting a small group or checking in with someone who's had a tough morning – how they shape the environment matters. Small tweaks can make a big difference.

Moments of Reflection

- 5.1 Interrelationships
- 5.2 Multiple Perspectives
- 5.3 Interrelationships
- 5.4 Curiosity
- 5.5 Multiple Perspectives
- 5.6 Practice
- 5.7 Interrelationships
- 5.8 Interrelationships
- 5.9 Practice
- 5.10 Interrelationships
- 5.11 Curiosity

References

Alloway, T. P., & Alloway, R. G. (2014). *Understanding working memory*. Sage Publications.

Department of Education. (2023). Headship national professional qualification. www.gov.uk/guidance/headship-national-professional-qualification

Department of Education & Department of Health and Social Care. (2014). SEND Code of Practice: 0 to 25 years. www.gov.uk/government/publications/send-code-of-practice-0-to-25

Education Endowment Foundation. (2018). Metacognition and self-regulated learning. https://educationendowmentfoundation.org.uk/education-evidence/guidance-reports/metacognition?utm_source=/education-evidence/guidance-reports/metacognition&utm_medium=search&utm_campaign=site_search&search_term=metacognit

Education Endowment Foundation. (2025). *Special educational needs in mainstream schools: Guidance report*. https://educationendowmentfoundation.org.uk/education-evidence/guidance-reports/send

Galaburda, A. M., & Sanides, F. (1980). Cytoarchitectonic organization of the human auditory cortex. Journal of Comparative Neurology, 190(3), 597–610. https://doi.org/10.1002/cne.901900311 [Accessed 13/02/25]

Merriam-Webster. (n.d.). Pedagogy. www.merriam-webster.com/dictionary/pedagogy

Nickerson, C. (2024). Schema theory in psychology. www.simplypsychology.org/what-is-a-schema.html

Paivio, A. (1971). *Imagery and verbal processes: A psychological model.* Holt, Rinehart and Winston.

Rosenshine, B. (2012). Principles of instruction. *American Educator.* www.teacher-toolkit.co.uk/wp-content/uploads/2018/10/Principles-of-Insruction-Rosenshine.pdf

Sherrington, T., & Caviglioli, O. (2020). *Teaching WalkThrus: Five-step guides to instructional coaching*. John Catt.

Sweller, J. (1988). Cognitive load during problem solving: Effects on learning. *Cognitive Science*, 12(2), 257–285. https://doi.org/10.1207/s15516709cog1202_4

6
The Whole Education Setting and Governance

Overview

This chapter considers the bigger picture, and depending on your role in an educational setting, some tasks may not feel relevant or you might not have access to the information. But it facilitates an overview of the boundaries in which you are working and helps identify **feedback loops** which are not only perhaps unhelpful to your own practice, but could also be symptomatic across the whole setting. It is an opportunity to step beyond your classroom's wall and consider the impact of governance which relates to system 5 in the VSM.

As practitioners, it can be easy to focus solely on the immediate demands of the classroom – lesson planning, learner needs, and daily routines. But the decisions made beyond the classroom walls by senior leadership shape the education environment.

This chapter begins by stepping back and considering how whole-setting initiatives are formed, communicated, and experienced across different layers of the organisation. Before whole-setting practices are considered, the players in governance and system 5 require consideration.

The flow of information, guidance and directives is evident in this top-down model, but what value is there in developing communication channels to flow in the opposite direction? What opportunities are there for the board to learn from the practitioners?

DOI: 10.4324/9781003400639-7

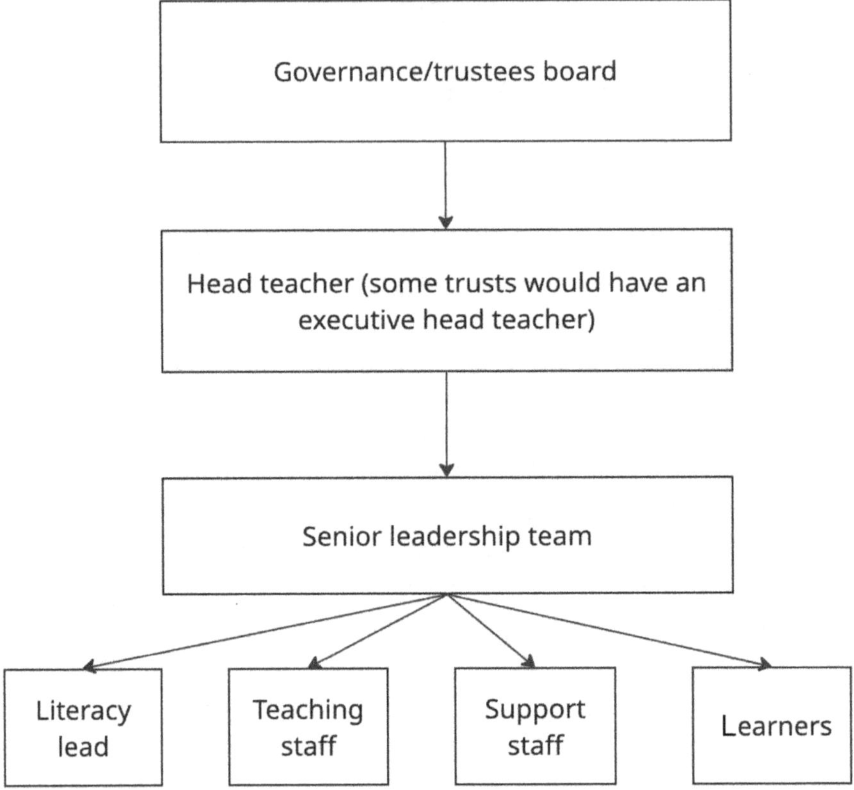

Figure 6.1 An organisation chart of an education setting

Moment of Reflection 6.1: Interrelationships

Use this example of an **organisational chart** to inform your system 5. Are there any additional players? What would be their scope of influence? How deep into the VSM system does this influence reach and is it reciprocal?

The purpose of this book is to encourage action and recognise the power that an individual – including both you as the practitioner and the learner – has to make changes. However, every person is an actor in a system and there are changes which can be made at an education setting level to support literacy across all subjects. This can also include an awareness of literacy in the setting including signage, communications and shared language. Whether you are a teaching assistant, a practitioner or in leadership this chapter outlines what can be achieved as a collective, and supports the class-based approach.

The case study below will be used to aid reflection throughout this chapter as much of the discussion is not related to classroom strategy. As you read through the chapter, consider the recommendations from the perspective of the newly qualified teacher (NQT) and how they would manage their boundaries in relation to new initiatives and what they will need to do in order to meet the requirements of governance whilst developing their own teaching style.

Case Study 3: An NQT Planning a New Topic with Literacy Integration

Background: Jordan Taylor, an NQT in their first year of teaching, responsible for a Year 4 class.

Primary Challenge: Planning a new cross-curricular topic that incorporates literacy skills while addressing the diverse learning needs of the learners and ensuring that the approach is in line with the setting's approach to teaching and learning.

Topic: 'Ancient Egypt' – integrating history, literacy and art.

Key Focus: Developing learners' literacy skills (reading, writing, speaking and listening) through engagement with the historical topic.

Key Challenges

Inexperience with Topic Planning:

- Curriculum Understanding: As a new practitioner, Jordan is still developing their knowledge of how to design and sequence lessons effectively across different subjects as well as ensure that the content reflects the planning provided by the setting. The education setting uses a traditional approach to curriculum planning which is based on mastery

of knowledge. Frequent knowledge checks to ensure that the learners are acquiring the right knowledge before moving on to the next topic.
- Balancing Content and Literacy: Unsure of how to incorporate literacy objectives within a history-based topic without overwhelming learners or sidelining key historical content.

Diverse Learner Abilities:

- Varied Literacy Levels: The class includes learners with a wide range of literacy abilities, from strong readers and writers to those struggling with basic reading comprehension and writing skills.
- Several learners have special educational needs (SEN) or English as an additional language (EAL), requiring differentiated approaches to literacy activities.

Limited Resources:

- Lack of Teaching Materials: As a new practitioner, Jordan lacks a bank of ready-made resources and must invest time in creating or sourcing materials for the topic.
- Time Management: Balancing lesson planning with other responsibilities as an NQT, including assessment and classroom management, is a challenge.

Systems Thinking Approach to Lesson Planning

Identifying Key Components

Core Literacy Skills: Jordan identifies key literacy objectives (e.g., reading comprehension, vocabulary development, narrative writing) to integrate into the Ancient Egypt topic.

Engaging Content: Planning to use the rich history of Ancient Egypt (myths, daily life, pharaohs) as a context for literacy activities, keeping the learners engaged and motivated.

Differentiated Learning: Recognising the need for differentiated tasks to meet the literacy needs of both higher- and lower-ability learners, as well as those with SEN or EAL.

Setting Clear Learning Objectives

Literacy Goals: Jordan establishes specific literacy objectives linked to the topic, such as:

- Reading: Understanding and analysing informational texts about Ancient Egypt.
- Writing: Writing a diary entry from the perspective of an ancient Egyptian learner or a pharaoh.
- Vocabulary: Expanding vocabulary with topic-specific words (e.g., hieroglyphs, pyramid, tomb, Nile).
- Speaking and Listening: Engaging learners in discussions and group work to develop oral language skills.

History Goals: Learning about the key aspects of Ancient Egyptian culture, including geography, society and famous figures.

Developing Strategies for Planning

Using Cross-Curricular Connections: Jordan plans to use the topic's historical content to create meaningful literacy tasks. For example:

- Reading Comprehension: Using texts about Ancient Egypt to practice retrieval and inference skills.
- Creative Writing: Learners write a short myth inspired by Egyptian mythology.
- Research Skills: Learners conduct research on a specific aspect of Ancient Egypt (e.g., mummification, pyramids) and create a fact file.

Differentiation:

- Providing texts with limited vocabulary, highlighting the key terms for the topic. Additional support, such as sentence starters and visual aids, to help learners access the material.
- Higher-Ability Learners: Offering more challenging texts and encouraging extended writing or independent research projects.

Utilising Available Resources:

- Text Selection: Jordan selects a range of texts on Ancient Egypt, including non-fiction books, picture books and online articles, ensuring they are age-appropriate and accessible.
- Collaborating with Colleagues: Reaching out to more experienced practitioners for advice and resource sharing, particularly those who have previously taught similar topics.
- Online Platforms: Utilising online resources, such as educational websites, to find reading comprehension activities, writing prompts and vocabulary exercises related to Ancient Egypt.
- Library Resources: Checking with the education setting librarian for topic-specific books and resources that can support both literary and historical understanding.

Incorporating Formative Assessment

- Baseline Assessment: At the start of the topic, Jordan plans to assess learners' reading comprehension and writing skills through a short, topic-related activity (e.g., answering questions about a short passage on the pyramids).
- Ongoing Assessment: Throughout the topic, Jordan uses quick writing tasks, comprehension quizzes, and group discussions to monitor progress in literacy skills.
- Differentiated Feedback: Providing tailored feedback based on each learner's needs, focusing on areas such as vocabulary usage, sentence structure, or clarity in writing.
- Engaging Learners with Active Learning: Small group work or problem-solving activities.
- Group Projects: Jordan plans for learners to work in small groups to research a particular aspect of Ancient Egypt and present their findings to the class, allowing for collaborative learning and oral communication practice.
- Interactive Learning: Incorporating activities like creating hieroglyphic art or building model pyramids while reinforcing literacy through written reflections or instructions.

Increased Confidence ↔ Improved Literacy: As learners engage in more accessible and creative literacy tasks, they gain confidence in their reading and writing abilities, leading to greater participation and skill development.

> **Moment of Reflection 6.2: Practice**
>
> How could Jordan support their learners to recognise their strengths during this task? Highlighting the specific roles they played and reinforcing the value of these skills across other subjects and not just this task.

Engagement ↔ Academic Progress: By linking literacy tasks to a high-interest topic, Jordan anticipates that learners will be more motivated to participate in reading and writing activities, promoting academic progress.

Implementation and Support

Structured Lesson Plans:

- Weekly Themes: Jordan structures the topic around weekly themes (e.g., gods and goddesses, mummies, daily life), with each week focusing on a different aspect of Ancient Egypt tied to a literacy objective.
- Clear Timelines: Outlining timelines for completing each component of the topic, ensuring that learners have time to develop their literacy skills while covering the historical content.

Teaching Assistant (TA) Involvement:

- Targeted Support: The TA works with smaller groups of learners, particularly those with SEN or EAL, to provide additional support with reading and writing tasks.
- Focus on Engagement: The TA helps manage group activities and ensures that learners who may struggle with focus are engaged and supported during literacy tasks.

Parental Involvement:

- Home Reading: Encouraging parents to support their learners by reading topic-related books at home, helping reinforce vocabulary and comprehension skills.

- Communication: Sending regular updates to parents about the topic and literacy goals, so they can support their children's learning at home.

Outcomes

Improved Literacy Skills:

- Reading Comprehension: Learners show increased engagement and understanding of the topic through improved reading comprehension, especially in summarising and inferring information from texts.
- Writing Confidence: Learners become more confident in their writing, especially when writing creatively or reflectively about Ancient Egypt.
- Vocabulary Expansion: Learners' use of topic-specific vocabulary increases, demonstrating their ability to incorporate new words into both speaking and writing tasks.

Increased Engagement with the Topic:

- Learners display greater interest in Ancient Egypt, contributing to more focused and engaged literacy activities.
- Interactive tasks (e.g., writing a myth, group presentations) help learners feel more connected to both the topic and their literacy learning.

Differentiated Learning Success:

- SEN and EAL learners show progress in literacy skills, with individualised support enabling them to participate meaningfully in both group and independent tasks.
- Higher-ability learners challenge themselves through extended writing and research projects, deepening their understanding of both the topic and literacy objectives.

How Reading and Text Is Treated in Education Settings Can Influence Habitual Reading

If a reading scheme is adopted this often means levels of books are used and this can mean some learners get stuck on a certain level or become fixated with completing all the levels. Neither is conducive to developing their reading skills. Reading should be a habit, but when it becomes a chore to be endured and finished as soon as possible it becomes unsustainable.

Sadly, not all education settings have librarians but consider the ideas here and how they might apply to your setting. Reflect on the similarities and differences and identify a couple of strategies which you might share and explore in your own setting.

Developing a Reading Habit

Habits take time and commitment to develop and with any habit that is good for us, often the initial stages of forming that habit can feel hard and the temptation to give up is strong.

As explored previously, if the skill of reading is hard, the chances of it being an enjoyable past-time are limited. Whilst the benefits of reading are known, and persevering with the little and often approach works, that can be easier said than done.

For developing readers, this implies that the skills of reading are not yet automatic and will therefore take up mental capacity which leaves less for understanding and enjoyment. There are books published by Barrington Stoke which are written by well-known authors with strict guidelines in relation to the vocabulary used and the complexity of the language. These books give learners and adults texts that they can read at their reading ability, but the content is age appropriate.

Moment of Reflection 6.3: Practice

Jordan has planned to make use of the library and identified the need for a range of reading material to support the class's reading ability. How could Jordan ensure that the diverse needs of their class are met through their choice of reading material?

The Important Role of the Librarian in Education

I was fortunate to work with the best librarian in the world and her dedication to children's literature was unparalleled. It wasn't just the books she sourced and carefully curated for the learners, but it was also her passion for books and making them as accessible as possible. She introduced QR codes as soon as they became available so learners could see videos of other learners talking about the book before borrowing them. She would hold author events and had a vast collection of picture books. Jenny Jones, Head Preparatory School Librarian, has shared some of her ideas with you here.

Dear practitioner,

Whenever a learner comes into the education setting library and I'm asked to find them a book, I always ask them two questions as starters.

1. *What book did you last read that you loved?*
2. *What are your interests generally?*

The first question tells me a lot of things. It can tell me about the reading ability of the learner in front of me without having to potentially shame them about what 'level' they are at. It tells me something about genre or the kind of book that they love to read. It tells me whether they even have a book that they loved (sometimes the answer is 'I've never loved a book', this is important to know) but best of all it usually starts our book search off with a happy memory. What book did you last read that you loved? The second question also appeals to pleasure and happiness. What interests you? What do you love in the wider world? Is it computer games, is it sport, is it pets etc. Because here's the thing about learners and reading. For most learners, learning to read is difficult. As hoary old adults we have long forgotten just how hard it was to drag ourselves through those seemingly endless reading schemes. It's hard, it's often boring (especially compared to all of the modern distractions out there) and it requires practice. 'A person's a person, no matter how small' as Dr Seuss wrote, and as people we need to know why we're doing something difficult that requires practice. We need to know that the reward for the struggle is worth it.

There's no point in telling learners of any age that it will improve their job prospects, get them better grades, help them access the curriculum or anything as abstract as that. Do you love Pokémon? Here's an Encyclopaedia of Pokémon and their evolutions, it's easier to browse than a website. Do you love football? Here's the life story of your favourite player. Do you like Minecraft? Here's a story set in the Minecraft world for you to get lost in. If (like my eldest son) you are five and interested in engineering, then here's a book of machine cross-sections. If you want to know what all of the parts are called and what they do, you're going to have to practise your reading skills! The effort will be worth it because you are engaging in your interests and your passions.

Most learners love funny, scary or exciting books. Don't we all? We crave high emotion, it's how we're wired as humans. The good news is that there are so many fabulous books being published all of the time for every age group that will trigger these high emotions. When we're competing for the attention of our learners with a gaming and entertainment industry that knows exactly how to keep them engaged, we need to rise to the challenge. Sitting still and focusing on a paper book takes practice. Putting sounds together to decode words is hard. Make the rewards for this effort immediate and obvious. Let them read comics. Let them read non-fiction. Let them read anything (age appropriate) that sets their hearts alight and defend a space and time in their day for them to do this in. These would be my pleas from my many years on the library desk.

Jenny

Moment of Reflection 6.4: Practice

What is your relationship with the librarian? Does your education setting have one? Do learners have dedicated library lessons? Is this focused on reading, or does it incorporate referencing and research skills?

What provision is made for those learners who struggle with reading?

Meeting the Needs of a Diverse Cohort

According to ADHD UK (2025) 1 in 9 people are likely to have ADHD based on population data. The *British Medical Journal* (2024) estimates that 1 in 100 children are diagnosed as autistic. It is considered by the British Dyslexia Association (n.d.), that 10% of the population are likely to be dyslexic and dyspraxia/DCD affects approximately 5–6% of the population (Zwicker et al., 2012).

Even an average of these figures would result in a wide range of needs in a classroom, yet less than a quarter of the population have a diagnosed difficulty. In classrooms the number of learners and young people struggling is likely to be far higher. If effort is put into seeking support for these learners, there is a risk of ignoring the bigger picture in the pursuit of answers.

Let's consider then what a framework for literacy might look like, and as this chapter is focused on a whole education setting approach this will be something that is broader than classroom practice. In the spirit of systems thinking, this framework must be iterative and embrace uncertainty; it needs to be resilient but flexible and offer enough flexibility to deal with unknowns or group-wide needs.

Moment of Reflection 6.5: Curiosity

Before reading on remind yourself of the reflections you made earlier in the book about SEND in your setting.

Does SEND have a set of classrooms in the setting? Is this available to all learners or certain ones? If the latter, how is this decision made? What impact does access to all or specific cohorts have on the setting as a whole?

Why Language Is Important in Systems Thinking and Why It Should Be Carefully Considered in the Education Environment

When beginning initiatives, it is important to be mindful of how they will land. Learners are aware of hierarchies in spite of innocuous names or coloured tables. They soon work out which table needs more support or is in receipt of differentiated work. It is important, therefore, as an education establishment to consider the whole education setting approach to SEND including its language.

Moment of Reflection 6.6: Practice

As Jordan plans to support those with learning differences, what would be your advice in regard to understanding their needs (apply your expertise but also what you have learnt about systems thinking)? Where should they look for further guidance? Is there a policy that they should be mindful of before applying any methods to differentiate their cohort?

Establishing Your Education Setting's Starting Point

In the same vein that you have analysed your own starting point and your cohorts, now consider the education setting as a whole. The following three frameworks will help you decide where you need to begin with the whole education setting literacy approach and which path to take.

As this book's intention is to support those that are struggling to access education for a myriad of reasons but predominantly related to SEND, the first step is to consider literacy. The next step on this phase of the framework is to consider the SEND provision alongside literacy and you will see it follows a similar pattern. When you have your answers to both of these sections, hopefully you will have an idea of what to focus on as an education setting or where the education setting would benefit from investing some resources. You might even have identified both a SEND and literacy need which can be implemented and monitored to see some immediate results.

Moment of Reflection 6.7: Interrelationships

Take a moment to reflect on your role, boundaries and recognised channels of communication in your setting.

Is it easy to share ideas across subjects?

How can you inform whole education setting practice?

Is there someone actively looking at innovation and how contactable are they to everyone on the staff body?

If you provided feedback to senior leaders, how do you think this feedback would be received?

Three areas need to align to support learning differences with literacy or SEND; Figure 6.2 shows a system which highlights the interrelationships between the outlined areas in the table that follows.

Systems thinking relies on curiosity and keeping an open mind so whilst this information gathering exercise is useful, the value here is in triangulating this information and looking for patterns.

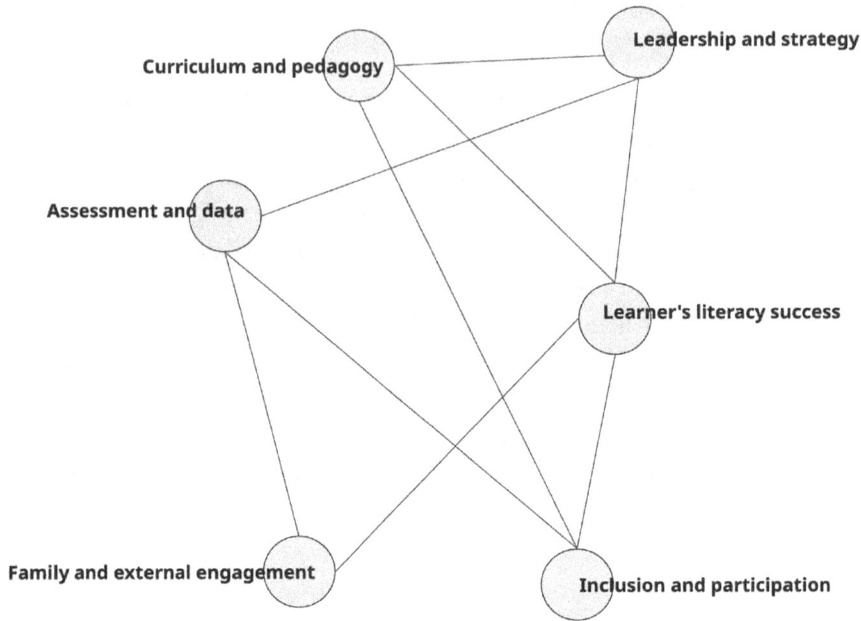

Figure 6.2 An education setting literacy, SEND and assessment system

Table 6.1 Whole education setting planning in three key areas

Literacy	*SEND*	*Assessment*
How is leadership addressed in whole education setting literacy planning?	What external support does the education setting use to identify and assess SEND?	What baseline assessments are used in your setting?
Is literacy embedded in subject plans?	How are parents and carers kept informed about a learner's assessment or support needs.	Where is the information held?

(*continued*)

Table 6.1 Continued

Literacy	*SEND*	*Assessment*
How explicit is literacy in meetings, planning and whole education setting delivery?	Do learners with SEND have access to ALL areas of the education setting?	How is it interpreted?
Do all practitioners feel confident in teaching literacy?	Do learners with SEND have clear next step plans for future study or work?	What literacy assessments are used?
Is there a named literacy leader?	Can they access the curriculum and thrive?	What scores are recorded? (standardised or reading ages)
	Is the SENCo visible on the senior leadership team (SLT) and contactable by all staff?	Is there a specialist teacher assessor on staff?

Looking for Patterns

When you have collated your answers to these questions, consider how the responses relate to each other and whether there are gaps that could be explored by teams to improve the interrelationships.

Governance and Influence

Once you have reflected upon literacy, SEND and assessment, consider how the governing body of your setting reviews, supports and challenges progress in all three areas.

As information flows between the classroom, SLT and Governance, consider where the points of delay or distortion might occur. Who receives the data and who interprets it?

Reflect on how the boundary judgements (who is excluded/included) affect the overall effectiveness of literary and/or inclusion strategies.

Moment of Reflection 6.8: Boundary Judgement

Reflect on a time when you or a colleague's boundary was challenged regarding their role. This might have been a voluntary overstepping of this boundary or a time when the boundary needed to be reinforced.

Developing a Reflective Practice

Reflecting on information, situations or events can be a bit nebulous and using a framework to support this such as the ones below can make the process of reflection more structured and intentional.

The following models will help support your evaluation. Whether that is of a specific intervention, your practice or the system as a whole.

Kolb's Experiential Cycle (McLeod, 2025b) is all about learning through experience by moving through four key stages: Concrete Experience, Reflective Observation, Abstract Conceptualisation and Active Experimentation.

It starts with a **Concrete Experience** – something you've done or encountered. From there, you step back and engage in **Reflective Observation**, considering what happened and identifying any patterns or key takeaways. Next, you move into **Abstract Conceptualisation**, where you make sense of the experience by connecting it to theories, principles or broader insights. Finally, you enter **Active Experimentation**, applying what you've learned to new situations and seeing how it plays out.

Kolb's model is great because it highlights that learning is an ongoing cycle, not a one-time event. It's especially useful for hands-on learning, coaching and leadership development because it helps turn everyday experiences into structured growth opportunities. Instead of just going through the motions, Kolb's cycle encourages intentional reflection and adaptation, making it a practical tool for continuous improvement.

Gibbs' Reflective Cycle (McLeod, 2025a) is a straightforward yet powerful framework for thinking through experiences, particularly in learning and professional development. It breaks reflection into six stages: Description, Feelings, Evaluation, Analysis, Conclusion and Action Plan.

Essentially, you start by describing what happened (without judgement), then move into how you felt during the experience. Next, you evaluate what worked and what didn't before analysing why things played out the way they did. From there, you draw conclusions about what you learned and, finally, create an action plan for how you'll approach similar situations in the future.

The beauty of Gibbs' model is that it forces you to slow down and consider experiences from multiple angles rather than just reacting. It's particularly useful in coaching, leadership and personal growth because it emphasises learning through cycles, ensuring that each reflection feeds into ongoing improvement. It's not just about dwelling on past events – it's about using them as a springboard for better decisions and actions moving forward.

After you have taken some time to consider the findings from your whole education setting analysis you may want to evaluate them and potentially share your findings with others in your setting.

As a way of achieving this, consider the following question.

1. What are the strengths and weaknesses we have identified?
2. Have you created a strategy to champion the successes and address the weaknesses?
3. Were there any training needs identified? And how can they be met?
4. Was the information you uncovered fit for purpose and relevant? Or do you need to reframe the questions you ask?
5. To what extent are things working well in your setting? And if they could be better, which stakeholders do you need to engage to make improvements?

The final model is by Peter Checkland, a pioneer of systems thinking and the creator of the **soft systems model**. This system's thinking model is related to causal maps but has not been covered in-depth during this book. The steps provide guidance to achieving a deeper level of evaluation (a reflexive practice as mentioned in Chapter 2) and incorporate multiple perspectives as well as an appreciation for uncertainty. CATWOE, which stands for Customers, Actors, Transformation, World View, Owner, Environmental constraints (Checkland & Scholes, 1990), encourages reflection from multiple perspectives as it works through the following steps.

You might like to try and address each of the questions in the first column in relation to a situation you wish to explore through the VSM. This might be related to your practice, a specific cohort or learner, or a strategy.

The benefits of **CATWOE** are it embeds the work on yourself and your values in evaluation. It might be worthwhile revisiting your reflections on values carried out in Chapter 2.

Table 6.2 CATWOE and how to use it to provide feedback on the VSM

CATWOE	Relation to VSM system
Customers	System 1
Who are the beneficiaries or victims of the system/process?	
Whose interests are affected (positively or negatively) by the transformation?	
Actors	System 1, 4 and 5
Who carries out the main activities within the system?	
Who is responsible for implementing the changes?	
Who would do the transformation?	
Transformation Process	System 1 and 3
What is the core transformation being performed?	
What is the input and what is the output?	
What is being changed from what, to what?	
Worldview	System 5 and the environment
What is the bigger picture or underlying worldview that makes this transformation meaningful?	
What beliefs, values and assumptions underpin the system?	
Why is this transformation important?	
Owner	System 1 and 5
Who has the power to start or stop the transformation?	
Who could abolish or change the system?	
Environmental Constraints	ALL systems
What external factors or limitations impact the system?	
What cannot be changed?	
What are the boundaries within which the system operates?	

In a systems-thinking classroom, feedback is not a single event and part of an ongoing cycle of learning, reflection and adaptation. Whilst the above models were chosen to evaluate interventions, they can provide a valuable approach to use with learners.

Combining Kolb's experiential learning cycle with Gibbs' reflective model allows learners and practitioners to move fluidly between action and analysis – observing what happened, how it felt, what influenced it and how to respond next time.

Together, these approaches build a dynamic, holistic model where reflection isn't just about improving a task but about understanding the **system** surrounding it – enabling practitioners to design interventions that are not only effective but sustainable and learner-centred.

Here are a couple of examples from a science practical and an English lesson using Kolb's and Gibbs' feedback models.

Experiment

Test how different materials affect the brightness of a bulb in a circuit.

Concrete Experience: The hands-on experiment
Description and Feelings: What did we do? How was it to collaborate in a group?
Evaluation: What worked well and what didn't?
Analysis and Abstract Conceptualisation: Why did some materials perform better? How did we manage roles in groups?
Action Plan: What would I do differently next time in both the experiment and the group work?

English Task

Learners write a persuasive letter to their headteacher arguing for a change they'd like to see in the education setting (e.g., better lunch options, more break time).

Concrete Experience: Writing and revising a letter.
Feelings and Evaluation: Was I confident in my argument? Did I use persuasive techniques well?

Analysis: What features made my writing stronger? How did my planning help or hinder?

Action Plan: Next time, I'll plan more thoroughly/use more emotive language.

Open Conversations and Valuing the Insights from All Parts of the Systems

After completing any evaluation, the challenge is how to make the most of what you have uncovered. This might result in needing to have a conversation with managers and leaders. This requires careful management as your findings could be viewed as criticism.

One approach which supports such conversations is coaching. The benefits to coaching are:

- Goal oriented
- Non-judgemental
- Structured and intentional
- Curious
- Collaborative

Coaching is highlighted as a worthwhile approach to training in The Reading Framework (Department of Education, 2021) and demonstrates an investment in long-term changes which might take a while to see the impact of rather than quick fixes. Whilst this guidance focuses on supporting literacy the principles can be applied across a wide range of subjects and situations. As a way to improve literacy in the classroom it recommends that those with responsibility for literacy should support their colleagues through coaching, and that practice and being able to apply strategies without fear of reprisal leads to growth.

Moment of Reflection 6.9: Practice

If Jordan was struggling to implement a suggested literacy strategy, how could they use the evaluation from CATWOE to broach the subject with their line manager?

A challenging chapter draws to a close which has explored systems of leaderships and how information is shared across the levels. It introduced a case study of an NQT and how they could learn to navigate the complex needs of their learners and identify feedback loops which might be unhelpful to both the development of their practice but also their learners. It has encouraged a deeper level of analysis relating to literacy, SEND and assessment which will hopefully inform your practice. It might also highlight systemic issues, which through careful and considerate feedback, you could use to affect change on a whole school level.

Moments of Reflection

- 6.1 Interrelationships
- 6.2 Practice
- 6.3 Practice
- 6.4 Practice
- 6.5 Curiosity
- 6.6 Practice
- 6.7 Interrelationships
- 6.8 Boundary Judgement
- 6.9 Practice

References

ADHD UK. (2025). *ADHD diagnosis rate in the UK*. https://adhduk.co.uk/adhd-diagnosis-rate-uk

British Dyslexia Association. (n.d.). Dyslexia. www.bdadyslexia.org.uk/dyslexia

British Medical Journal. (2024). Autism spectrum disorder. www.bma.org.uk/what-we-do/population-health/improving-the-health-of-specific-groups/autism-spectrum-disorder

Checkland, P., & Scholes, J. (1990). *Soft systems methodology in action*. John Wiley & Sons.

Department for Education. (2021). *The reading framework: Teaching the foundations of literacy*. www.gov.uk/government/publications/the-reading-framework-teaching-the-foundations-of-literacy

McLeod, S. (2025a). Gibbs reflective cycle. www.simplypsychology.org/gibbs-reflective-cycle.html

McLeod, S. (2025b). Kolb's learning styles and experiential learning cycle. www.simplypsychology.org/learning-kolb.html

Zwicker, J. G., Missiuna, C., Harris, S. R., Boyd, L. A. (2012). Developmental coordination disorder: A review and update. European Journal of Paediatric Neurology, 16(6), 573–581. https://doi.org/10.1016/j.ejpn.2012.05.005

7

Support Strategies to Progress Learning

Overview

This chapter's focus is on practical strategies to support learning in the classroom. It takes into consideration the cognitive skills of language, processing and working memory which were discussed in Chapter 5, and provides ways to address reading, writing and spelling difficulties. Whilst some of the strategies may suit different ages of learners, the majority can be tweaked to suit the age of a learner. It combines expertise from both class practitioners and literacy specialists to identify classroom strategies to support learners with additional learning challenges.

As you read through the strategies, consider how they might inform your practice and how they would impact your classroom. As you reflect on the different strategies, evaluate them for their appropriateness and suitability for your setting.

Supporting literacy development in the classroom isn't about finding a perfect strategy, it's about building a toolkit that can evolve and flex in response to learners. This chapter brings together a wide range of practical, research-informed approaches to support reading, writing, spelling and memory. Whether you're stacking strategies, adapting your environment, or rethinking how information is shared, the aim here is not to fix but to scaffold.

Scaffolds for When the Learning Curve Feels Too Steep

Stacking uses lots of different strategies without considering one as the fix-all approach. It requires a holistic approach and lots of strategies to

DOI: 10.4324/9781003400639-8

draw from. It also means looking at each learner in detail to identify which options would work for them. This combination of strategies could be unique to that learner but encompass ways which work for others. The intention is to find the combination which works best for that individual and they can then use them in other areas of their life. For example, a learner with dyslexia may struggle to copy from the board and require a paper copy of the notes in front of them and use these notes to highlight and discuss. Another learner may also need the notes but benefit from copying them into their book or type them up. Stacking strategies draws on the **Universal Design for Learning (UDL)** framework (https://udlguidelines.cast.org), **cognitive load theory**, and **multisensory teaching** principles. By combining support across domains – rather than relying on one 'fix' – the pressure is reduced on the learner's weakest areas while strengthening engagement, confidence and access to learning.

None of the recommended strategies in the image below are intended for a specific difficulty but could be applied for a number of different needs such as shorter attention spans or vocabulary challenges or difficulties following verbal information. They are all intended to be used in conjunction with one another and therefore the frequency and need for the strategies will depend upon the user.

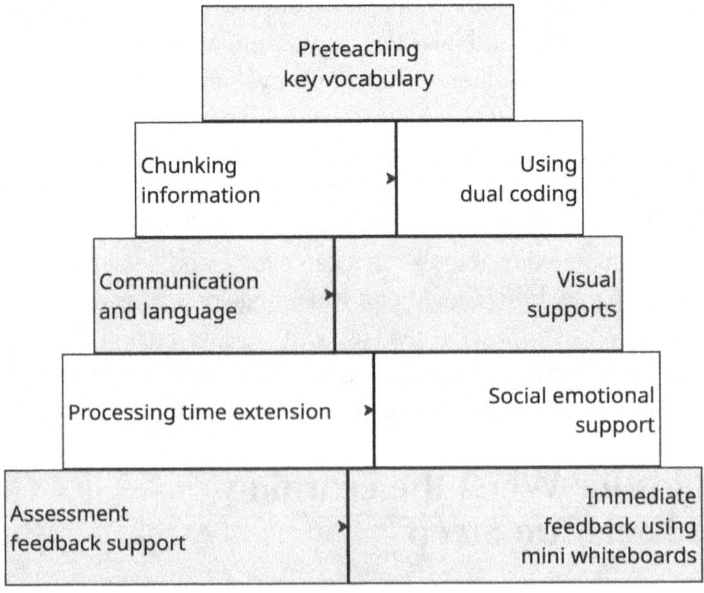

Figure 7.1 Stacking interventions

Moment of Reflection 7.1: Practice

Make a list of the strategies you already use to support your cohorts and consider which ones would work well together. How would they work if they were stacked? Do some of your strategies only work alone and have limited scope and therefore cannot be mapped to your day-to-day planning?

Classroom Strategies: The Set-Up

Considering the environment and the impact that it may have on the learners means reflecting upon what is inside and outside of your control. For example, you might not be able to prevent the smells of lunch from the canteen if your classroom is next to the lunch hall but you can reflect on the tasks you set at certain times of the day and how the environment might impact the intended outcome. Similarly, if you share a classroom you might not be able to control what is on the walls as displays or how the tables are arranged. You can decide on who sits next to whom and ensure you are aware of the room's blind spots, distracting noises and seats which are hemmed in and difficult to move from swiftly if needed. These are not the places to assign to the most anxious of learners.

Moment of Reflection 7.2: Multiple Perspectives

You might want to carry out an audit of your classroom to really understand the environment and understand what might reduce a cohort's focus through no fault of their own or your teaching.

Consider all of the following:

- Seating: Comfort, accessibility, cleanliness, sight of the board, proximity to the door
- Windows: Sun direction, on the board, on you, on the learners
- Overhead lighting: Is it harsh and causing glare on white paper?
- Temperature: How manageable is this?

- Resources: Accessible, available and offered in different forms such as electronic and on paper?
- Proximity and location in relation to the rest of the setting: Up a flight of stairs, furthest from the gates, near the canteen, etc.

Information Sharing and Communication

After considering the classroom environment, the focus turns to how you share information.

If you have been completing the VSM over the course of the book, consider adding a block to system 2 (communication) as you will have been populating system 1 with WHAT you do but now the attention is turned to how it is communicated.

There are several factors related to communication and the first is language. If you share information through a whiteboard – and this could be handwritten or through an interactive whiteboard or a visualiser – how accessible is that information?

Moment of Reflection 7.3: Practice

Are you expecting the learners to copy down the information?

If you are, for what purpose?

Are you demonstrating something?

And if so, what are the learners doing at the time?

Are they watching or taking notes?

Is there a way of sharing information which is accessible on a digital platform at the same time so that individuals can either follow the information or focus on specific elements safe in the knowledge they can revisit the full version later at home?

Consider the content of what you're writing. Are you making instruction words explicit? Have you used headings which they can then use in their writing?

Are you explaining any key words?

Does the class understand the terminology being used or do you need to scaffold their understanding of the language which you are using?

The Value of Being a Practitioner

Knowledge transfer is a significant element of learning, and the direction of this transfer remains mainly from the teacher to the pupils; the expert to the novice. When knowledge is shared in a meaningful way by passionate practitioners, this knowledge can stay with you for life. I was fortunate to have a psychology teacher, Mrs. W, who was not only passionate about her subject but was an unapologetic champion of all her learners. She applied her knowledge of the subject to support us in building the strategies in order to remember the specific details of studies and experiences, many of which I still remember today. Her methods were not limited to the subject of psychology and her learning strategies could be applied across many subjects. She taught with love and compassion but above all else, the belief her learners could achieve.

It is not only teachers who can have such an impact on learners, and my eldest daughter fondly remembers her English teaching assistant who provided her with the emotional support she needed to get through the day. Again, it was love and support which was the foundation of this relationship.

Teaching assistant Harriett Booth shares her words of wisdom for practitioners here. Harriet and I met when she attended a series of round tables about SEND and dyslexia. We shared values in understanding the individual in the classroom and how important a reflective, holistic approach is.

Moment of Reflection 7.4: Practice

As you read through Harriet's letter, consider the opportunities in your practice to explore what learning is and how to create an environment that supports curiosity and reflection about the process of learning itself.

Dear practitioner,

Greetings from a Teaching Assistant!

If you're classroom based, I do hope you are fortunate enough to have a teaching assistant (TA) working with you.

I've worked in a lot of classes, with many different styles of great teaching and a fantastic range of learners with every imaginable learning style. The memorable ones? Where everyone's skills are explicitly valued; where it's fine to 'not get' something and where individual progress is celebrated over highest-score-in-the-class. Where learners, only some of whom may perhaps remind you of cautious woodland creatures who need coaxing out to join in, begin to believe in themselves as learners, develop a 'have-a-go' attitude, and begin to trust you to help them believe in their own abilities.

Teaching assistants... or assistant practitioners? We've come a long way from sharpening pencils and hearing readers...

Much of my work feels like listening and talking, with an emphasis on listening. Even before I became an SEN support TA (Speech and Language and SpLD), listening was crucial to find out what was really blocking a learner. I know – time for the soft skills can sometimes feel like a luxury in the swirling mass of different needs and abilities in mainstream classes where every practitioner now needs to be an SEN expert as well as everything in the job description and more. But that, apparently inconsequential, chat often throws up the missing pieces in a learner's emotional and intellectual landscape that's crucial to unravelling whatever they're struggling with. Often, it feels like breaking cycles. Learner not reading at home? – useful to bear in mind 1 in 6 adults in England are functionally illiterate (National Literacy Trust, n.d.). And to remind ourselves of the everyday impact of not being able to read. It's a corner worth fighting – trying to ensure explicit reading instruction/appropriate tech is provided for those struggling at any key stage to keep up with the reading demands in an education setting and dispelling the myth that once you've mastered phonics, you're sorted.

Memories of an education setting and learning can be viscerally powerful (Channel 4 Entertainment) and influence our approach as practitioners. The subject we loved or agonised over? It all informs our practice. Learning a new language and taking up a new sport provided me with a humbling reminder of what it is like to struggle, get stuck, give up for a while (aka take a break) and have another go. No bad thing, I think...

So here's a cheer from me to you, for acting as a buffer between your learners and whatever demands the current curriculum policy makes, for your empathy, your flexibility within the clear behaviour expectation boundaries that create an environment for learning... and a learning habit for life.

From Harriett

Moment of Reflection 7.5: Multiple Relationships

If you are a teacher and work with a teaching assistant, what are their values and how do they impact the class? What space are they given to develop their practice in your classroom?

If you are a teaching assistant, are there opportunities for you to give feedback on classroom practices and how to better meet the needs of the children you work with?

Vocabulary and Communication

As the focus on communication is continued, the attention is turned to vocabulary.

Idioms and sayings in everyday language can cause confusion for some learners. As can less common vocabulary.

Beck et al. (2013) devised a hierarchy of vocabulary called **The Three Tiers of Vocabulary**. This was to support the acquisition of tier two words which have been identified as being a marker of progress in literacy.

Table 7.1 The three tiers of vocabulary (Beck et al., 2013)

Tier One:

These are everyday words and high frequency words. Often a learner with literacy difficulties will rely heavily on these words and sometimes they remain challenging to read and spell throughout their life. They need consistent rehearsal before they become automatically known.

Tier Two:

These words are the ones which have a lot of capital in written work. They elevate a text and add richness and depth. They are the product of lots of reading and accessing a wide range of texts. If you find reading hard, you are unlikely to read as much as someone who finds it easy and therefore you miss out on the opportunity to develop your vocabulary. They can also be harder to spell and therefore sticking to words which are familiar feels much more comfortable.

Tier Three:

These are subject-specific and technical terms. There are numerous terms in mathematics and science, and these can be really difficult to both read and spell. They are necessary to understand technical subjects, but they are not as transferable as tier one or tier two words and therefore their usefulness is limited to the subject.

Vocabulary goes hand in hand with reading fluency and an exposure to text. These elements combined make for successful readers. This is related to written text which is the most popular medium for text in education settings currently but is the most challenging for those with dyslexia. Try to identify alternative ways to explore vocabulary, for example through debate or discussions.

Moment of Reflection 7.6: Curiosity

Where are there opportunities to explore vocabulary in my practice with the learners and introduce tier 2 words to broaden their vocabulary?

Could discussion or debate be introduced to some lessons to work on speaking and listening skills?

Memory and Retention

The more of the brain you can engage when learning new material; the better.

Creating lots of hooks for new material by varying the approach used will make it more memorable.

Here are a few suggestions for varying the approach to information regardless of the subject or topic:

- Prioritising – rating the information from 1 to 5; e.g., which wife did Henry 8th love the most?
- Colour coding – this must be repeated and where possible used in their books.
- Categorising – putting information into groups. These can be meaningful like rulers of England or personal to the learner. These build on the idea of schema, covered in more detail here.
- Writing out notes and condensing them until you have keywords which then trigger the main information.

These strategies all activate different neural pathways and encourage the brain to process the information using different methods which make it more memorable.

Barrett's taxonomy (Educational Taxonomies, 2014) also supports this curious and scaffolded approach to exploring knowledge. The information remains the same, but the method of questioning is altered to stretch and deepen a learner's understanding of the information. Barrett's taxonomy uses a variety of approaches and subsequent related questions.

Table 7.2 Barrett's taxonomy (Educational Taxonomies, 2014)

Recognition/Recall	What information was shared? Who was involved, and what did they do?
Reorganisation	How would you summarise the key points in your own words? Can you organise what happened into a timeline or list?
Inferential	What can you work out that wasn't directly said? What clues suggest how someone might have felt or what might happen next?
Evaluation	What do you think worked well and what could have been better? Do you agree with the choices or actions taken? Why or why not?
Appreciation	What part stood out to you, and why do you think that is? How did this make you feel, and what does that tell you about your values?

Below is an example of how Barrett's taxonomy can be used to revise the topic of rivers in geography.

Table 7.3 An application of Barrett's taxonomy

Recognition/Recall	Describe or draw the main points of a river
Reorganisation	Consider similarities/differences to other bodies of water. Explore cause and effect
Inferential	Explain the key points and evaluate them on their significance to the environment around the river
Evaluation	What do you think are the main challenges rivers face today?
Appreciation	Is there anything that is surprising or makes you feel a certain way? How would you feel living by a river?

Moment of Reflection 7.7: Practice

Apply Barrett's taxonomy to a task you have planned to add additional reinforcement and increase the retention of the shared information.

Education is about constructing a body of knowledge and demonstrating your understanding of it at various points along your educational journey. For learners and young people, however, the content is typically selected by others, which can make engaging with the material even more challenging – unlike as adults, when you have the freedom to choose your courses.

As discussed earlier in Chapter 5, memory capacity varies from person to person. If you struggle with memory or processing, retaining and recalling information can be even more difficult.

Taking a systems thinking approach to knowledge transfer, it is important to consider how active a learner is in their acquisition of knowledge.

Imagine encountering a new topic that contains specific information essential for understanding it. The way in which that information is presented and the timing are critical to its retention. Below are some strategies to reduce the load on your working memory and maximise long-term retention:

- **Minimise Distractions:** When introducing new information, eliminate unnecessary distractions. Turn off extraneous noise, colours, and images that aren't directly relevant – these can be added later to create meaningful associations. At this stage, focus on establishing a clear understanding before embedding the material deeply.
- **Encourage Active Engagement:** Involve learners actively in their learning by having them summarise the material to each other. They might create bullet points or explain the concepts back to you to reinforce their comprehension.
- **Streamline the Material:** Reduce the overall amount of information to be stored by shortening sentences or limiting the number of items that need to be remembered.
- **Teach Key Extraction Techniques:** Show learners how to extract and focus on essential details from what they hear or read, thereby

reducing information overload. Summarising is a valuable revision tool – for example, the **Cornell note-taking** system helps learners concentrate on key information without the pressure to record every detail.

- **Regular Review:** Schedule frequent reviews of new material, giving opportunities to overlearn key facts until they become automatic.
- **Use Visual Strategies:** Adopt visual learning techniques by developing picture codes in your notes. Use diagrams, charts, and mind maps to create links between concepts. Encourage forming mental images or even drawing sketches in the margins and consider transforming text into a narrative or visual story to enhance retention.

By implementing these strategies, you can help mitigate the challenges of processing new information and foster a more effective learning environment.

Moment of Reflection 7.8: Interrelationships

As you read through the following case study, identify opportunities where Jay could be supported by their peers and how could this be facilitated. Are there occasions where Jay could excel? For example, being nominated scribe, or suggest tasks which work to their strengths?

Case Study 4: A Learner Who Finds It Difficult to Access Small Group Work

Background: 8-year-old learner, Jay, in a mainstream primary school.

Primary Challenge: Jay struggles with small group work due to social anxiety, communication difficulties, and difficulty maintaining focus in group settings. Their skills lie in art, and they are an excellent story writer.

Impact: Jay avoids participating in group tasks, leading to a lack of engagement with peers, limited collaboration skills, and missed opportunities to benefit from peer learning.

Key Challenges

Social Anxiety:

- Fear of Judgment: Jay is afraid of making mistakes in front of peers, which increases anxiety in small group settings.
- Avoidance: Tends to withdraw during group activities, letting others take the lead or choosing to work independently when possible.

Communication Difficulties:

- Reluctance to Speak: Jay struggles to express their ideas confidently in group discussions and is hesitant to contribute, leading to limited participation.
- Difficulty Understanding Group Dynamics: Jay finds it hard to follow fast-paced conversations or take turns, which results in frustration and further withdrawal.

Moment of Reflection 7.9: Practice

How can the soft skills of understanding group dynamics be taught explicitly to support Jay and the rest of the class with these key life skills?

Focus and Attention:

- Easily Distracted: Jay finds it hard to concentrate in group settings where multiple voices or activities are happening at once.
- Difficulty Sharing Attention: Struggles to follow group instructions and balance their focus between their work and listening to others.

Peer Interaction:

- Limited Social Skills: Jay has difficulties initiating interactions or negotiating roles within the group, resulting in feelings of isolation even within small groups.

- Conflict Avoidance: Prefers to avoid potential conflict by staying silent or agreeing with others, even if they disagree or feel confused about the task.

Systems Thinking Approach to Intervention

Identifying Key Leverage Points:

- Social Skills Development: Focus on improving Jay's ability to engage with others, starting with one-to-one interaction before progressing to small groups.
- Structured Group Work: Introducing clear roles and routines in group activities to give Jay more structure and predictability, reducing their anxiety.
- Practitioner/TA Support: Extra support during group activities to help Jay feel more confident and engaged.

Developing Strategies:

- Gradual Exposure: Start with pairs and gradually introduce small groups, ensuring that Jay builds confidence with fewer peers before working in larger groups.
- Clear Group Roles: Assign specific roles in group work (e.g., 'recorder', 'spokesperson') so that Jay knows exactly what is expected of them and feels more secure.
- Use of Visuals: Providing visual prompts or cues (e.g., task cards, turn-taking visuals) to help Jay understand the group's expectations and remain focused.

Modifying the Education Setting System:

- Practitioner and Peer Education: The practitioner educates the class about inclusive group work, encouraging peers to include Jay and give them space to contribute.
- Flexible Grouping: Allowing Jay to choose their group or work with familiar peers to reduce anxiety about interacting with less familiar classmates.
- Smaller Groups or Paired Work: Reducing group sizes to two or three learners at first to ease Jay into collaborative settings.

Addressing Feedback Loops:

- Confidence ↔ Participation: Increasing Jay's confidence through gradual exposure leads to more participation, which in turn builds further confidence.
- Positive Peer Interaction ↔ Engagement: Successful social interactions with peers reinforce positive feelings about group work, encouraging more engagement in future tasks.
- Reduced Anxiety ↔ Academic Progress: As Jay feels more comfortable in group settings, their anxiety decreases, which allows them to focus better and make more academic progress.

Implementation and Support

Practitioner Support:

- The practitioner provides regular feedback and encouragement during group tasks, reinforcing Jay's small successes to boost their confidence.
- Structured group work with clear instructions and roles, allowing Jay to focus on specific contributions rather than feeling overwhelmed.

Targeted Interventions:

- Social Skills Training: Regular sessions to teach Jay how to initiate conversations, take turns, and express their ideas in a group context.

Teaching Assistant Support:

- During group activities, the TA provides close support to Jay, prompting them to contribute and helping them stay focused when distractions occur.
- Gradually reducing the level of TA support as Jay gains confidence and becomes more independent in group work.

Outcomes

Increased Participation in Group Work:

- Over time, Jay becomes more comfortable contributing to small group tasks, particularly when roles are clearly defined, and expectations are structured.
- Jay starts participating in group discussions more regularly, offering their ideas with encouragement and support from the practitioner.

Improved Communication Skills:

- Jay gains confidence in speaking up during group activities, using the communication strategies learned through SALT and social skills training.
- Their ability to listen to others, wait for their turn and respond appropriately in group settings improves.

Social Integration:

- As Jay becomes more engaged in group work, they begin to form stronger connections with their peers, reducing feelings of isolation.
- Positive peer interactions increase, helping Jay feel more included in social and academic aspects of school life.

Reduced Anxiety:

- Through structured support and gradual exposure, Jay's anxiety about group work decreases, leading to better focus and participation.
- Jay develops greater resilience in handling group dynamics, making them more adaptable to different group settings.

Moment of Reflection 7.10: Practice

Reflect on a learner who has similar anxieties about group work and write down the strategies you have used in the past to support them. Are there any strategies which have been included in the case study that you would try in the future?

Multisensory Learning

Multisensory learning is frequently recommended for learners with literacy difficulties. It creates hooks for learning as it adds layers to information through the use of visual and auditory information. It provides variety which increases the interest level for the learner and stimulation of the brain.

Some ideas for multisensory learning have already been explored through the book but here are a few reminders. Dual coding, which is adding visual cues to written information. The use of colour to highlight important information. Varying the delivery of information so it is sometimes verbally presented. Giving learners the opportunity to discuss their ideas before writing them down. Using diagrams and mind mapping to explore ideas and revise information.

Moment of Reflection 7.11: Practice

What multisensory techniques can I incorporate into lessons?

How can I assess the effectiveness of these techniques in improving learner outcomes?

Reading Strategies: Providing Scaffolds for One of the Most Important Skills in Learning

If a learner is unable to access a text, they will find learning in the current education system challenging. The majority of information that is shared in education settings is text based and whilst this might be supplemented by visual information and practical tasks, the majority is text and a learner's response to this information is predominantly a written answer. Much of what is consumed in society is visual but this is not reflected in the curriculum that remains heavily text based. Learners today are having to code switch from one medium to another and there is less time spent socially developing their reading skills.

When you find reading difficult, you become stuck at the decoding phase. All text will require a high level of processing as not all the words will be automatically known; this results in less capacity to process that information for meaning. It will also reduce the potential for that information to be stored and recalled at a later date. Learners who find reading fluently hard have not reached a level of ease with text to 'break the rules of reading' and will approach each text with the same level of focus.

For the Young Emergent Readers

Know which sounds the learner has been learning and practise them before they start reading.

Look at the cover and help the learner guess what the book might be about.

Read the same book more than once so they can start to get a feel for being more fluent when reading.

Make a note of the words which they found tricky but worked out and praise them the next time they read that word without faltering.

When they tire, stop. The most important thing is for them to enjoy reading.

For Free Readers

Use the five-finger rule when choosing books – if a learner makes more than five errors on an average page in a new book it is too hard for them.

Reading is reading and that includes websites, newspapers, magazines and blogs. Books can be intimidating, especially to reluctant readers, so think of alternative mediums.

Give the learner a realistic expectation of how many pages they should read.

Encourage reading out loud to check their accuracy as poor reading habits are hard to break.

When they do come across a tricky word, remind them of the decoding skills they used before they became a free reader; they may still need to use these from time to time.

Echo Reading

Reading fluency takes time and practice and often relies on reading aloud which for a learner with literacy difficulties feels like the worst thing on earth to do, especially in front of other people. Echo reading, where the practitioner or parent reads a couple of lines and the learner repeats them and tries to copy the adult's intonation and rhythm, removes the pressure of reading the words correctly and places the emphasis on fluency instead.

For an Older Learner

It's important to still hear them read to ensure they're not skim reading or making too many misinterpretations, but preferably keep this activity to a one-to-one session away from their peers.

Ask them to summarise the chapter they have read whilst you flick through it yourself.

Encourage them to make predictions about what will happen next. Help develop inference from the text they are reading rather than just recalling information in the text.

Get them to elaborate on the characters. Would they choose them as a friend? What characteristics do they admire/dislike in the character?

Use quick reads of the classics to support reading a set text in class. You can apply Barrett's questions here to encourage a more robust discussion of the text.

Whole class readers can facilitate discussion and allow a learner who struggles with reading to show how much they can comprehend orally. However, a practitioner may think that building suspense and reading the books chapter by chapter allows the element of surprise to build.

If this is considered through the eyes of a learner who struggles to process the words as individual components, they are not absorbing the story and plot as they are focused on the writing at a text level. The effort is consumed by understanding how to decode the words and therefore the power of the writing is lost. Quite simply they lose the thread of the story because their reading ability fragments passages too much.

For learners to get the most out of a shared text they need to appreciate the story as a whole BEFORE they embark on the chapters in class. Ideally, a shortened, summarised version of the text is the best approach closely followed by the audio and finally a video. The familiarity with the text will empower a learner that struggles with reading. It will enable them to take part in discussions on various themes, plot lines and overcome the fear that they have of the words in the sentence. This facilitates a learner demonstrating their underlying ability rather than being hampered by the mechanics of reading.

Moment of Reflection 7.12: Curiosity

Identify the readability of your subject's texts by working out the readability score. This can be achieved using a Flesh-Kincaid test (https://readable.com/readability/flesch-reading-ease-flesch-kincaid-grade-level) or can also probably be achieved through cutting and pasting a few passages into a large language model. If the subject includes lots of technical language the score is likely to be higher and the need for additional support to learn these key terms will increase.

Writing Strategies

One of the most challenging aspects of education is getting your ideas down on paper. The effort required to generate the ideas, organise them and write the words can feel monumental. When you add to that a difficulty with spelling or handwriting, the task itself becomes secondary, and all focus shifts to accuracy. When you feel paralysed by spelling a word correctly you suspend the creative process, and kickstarting back into action is harder every time it is interrupted.

One of the best ways for learners to support the writing process is through discussion, but this can be limited and controlled by the practitioner in a way which reduces its potential to support a learner's productivity.

Below are more suggestions for supporting the writing process.

- Make use of **graphic organisers**; these can be designed by the practitioner and given out at the beginning of the project or added to by the learners throughout the topic, depending on the purpose of the organiser.
- Give time to talk through ideas for writing before starting.

- Use word banks and sentence starters to support the fear of the blank page.
- Try using a draft system to focus on one sub skill at a time. For example, capture ideas in the first draft, consider punctuation and/or sentence structure in the second, and on adding interesting vocabulary and extending descriptive language in the final draft.

Moment of Reflection 7.13: Practice

What options for recording information are available to your learners now? Do they meet the needs of the learners in your classroom and how do you know this?

Spelling Support

Spelling is a tough nut to crack. It can remain a difficulty when all other literacy skills improve. Adult life is full of cheats to get around the tricky task of writing words correctly. However, whilst there remains an emphasis on accurate spelling and punctuation, support is needed to develop word awareness.

There is no one way to teach spelling and not all approaches suit every learner.

1. Make a **mnemonic** up for tricky words, like Big Elephants Can Always Use Small Exits, and Never Eat Crisps Eat Salad Sandwiches And Remain Young.
2. Find spelling list words in reading books and spell them together in the air. Make sure your learner knows the meaning of the words they are learning to spell. Where might they come across the spellings in their everyday life?
3. Little and often is key. Limit spelling activities to five to ten minutes a day but do repeat key words regularly. Repetition is so important to learners who struggle with spelling as it takes much longer for their brains to store these words and recall them automatically.
4. Find words within words and encourage learners to be word detectives.

5. Use colour or symbols for really sticky words – increased exposure to these words, especially if they are high frequency words, will help automate spelling them.
6. Encourage **subvocalising** when spelling words. This will link auditory, motor, sequential and visual memory.
7. Explore new vocabulary using the root word, **prefix** and **suffix** approach to extend word knowledge and make this knowledge transferable to other subjects or word categories.

Moment of Reflection 7.14: Curiosity

What are the key reading and writing strategies my learners need to learn?

How can I model these strategies effectively in my teaching?

The classroom is a system, not a script, and neither the environment nor the people's interaction in it are fixed. Each learner will bring their own mix of strengths and challenges. This chapter explored ways to scaffold reading, writing and spelling and suggested frameworks such as stacking, Universal Design for Learning and multisensory teaching. These strategies can be added to the viable systems model, but the key is iteration and small adjustments to meet the needs of the learners.

None of the strategies are the key to an inclusive classroom but an invitation to adapt, reflect and respond.

Moments of Reflection

- 7.1 Practice
- 7.2 Multiple Perspectives
- 7.3 Practice
- 7.4 Practice
- 7.5 Multiple Perspectives
- 7.6 Curiosity
- 7.7 Practice

- 7.8 Interrelationships
- 7.9 Practice
- 7.10 Practice
- 7.11 Practice
- 7.12 Curiosity
- 7.13 Practice
- 7.14 Curiosity

References

Beck, I. L., McKeown, M. G., & Kucan, L. (2013). *Bringing words to life: Robust vocabulary instruction* (3rd ed.). Guilford Press.

Channel 4 Entertainment. (n.d.). *The write offs: Tackling dyslexia head-on.* www.youtube.com/watch?v=yFBMAAzXeks

Educational Taxonomies. (2014). Barrett taxonomy. https://educationaltaxonomy.weebly.com/home/barrett-taxonomy

National Literacy Trust. (n.d.). Adult literacy. https://literacytrust.org.uk/parents-and-families/adult-literacy

8
When Specialist Support Is Needed

Overview

This chapter explores the point at which classroom interventions are no longer enough and additional, specialist input becomes necessary. It reframes professional reports and EHCPs not as bureaucratic hurdles, but as part of a broader support system rooted in understanding each learner through multiple perspectives.

As evident throughout the book, you are encouraged to remain curious, to notice patterns, track emerging needs and reflect on what you know (and don't yet know) about your learners. Included is a detailed case study on applying for an EHCP demonstrating the emotional, legal and systemic navigation required throughout the process.

Whilst the focus of this book is on action and enabling practitioners to analyse their approach and understand their classroom on a deeper level, there are some learners who need more than classroom intervention, and their needs demand specific and often additional support. Some learners will require the involvement of outside agencies which will advise the practitioner on what needs to be implemented to safeguard that learner or support their learning. It is without question that such advice needs to be implemented but this can in itself be a challenge when the demands for such changes exceed one or two in a cohort.

DOI: 10.4324/9781003400639-9

Moment of Reflection 8.1: Practice

What information do you have to hand regarding your cohorts? Are you aware of their individual circumstances, and how is this reported or shared with you?

On a scale of 1–5 (1 being no impact and 5 being individual curriculum) how much of an impact do the specialist report or recommendations have on the classroom and planning?

Professional Reports and Their Application in the Classroom

Professional reports often include several recommendations and some of these may span that learner's education from their current age to university or the workplace. Specific learning difficulties reports are lifelong, and therefore they need a wide range of recommendations, which makes the practitioner's role even more challenging as they will need to discern which recommendations should take priority.

If whilst reading this book you have been completing the reflections and tasks, you should by now have a system of support that is built on multiple perspectives, interrelationships and understanding of individual differences. Applying guidance from specialist reports or EHCPs should follow the same pattern.

As a practitioner, you may or may not have access to the original reports; you may only be made aware that a learner has one and be given their diagnosis. If this is the case, you may need to liaise with your SENCo to find out the following information. It is recommended that you read any reports that a learner has, especially if you are unclear on what their diagnosis is. The reports should be kept on file by the SEND departments of your setting.

Identifying Additional Needs in the Classroom

There will be times when you will be the person who recognises a learner is finding something challenging in the classroom and this challenge is **persistent** but often **inconsistent** in its presentation. The learner might have good days where their learning flows and other days where they need more support from the outset – with understanding the task, recording their answers and recognising their errors.

If you have checked with the SEND department and they have no record of the learner, it will be important to monitor their progress and look for patterns.

The referral process will be different from one setting to another but below are recommended steps following the **Code of Practice** and the Assess, Plan, Do, Review cycle introduced earlier in Chapter 3. It is important to be mindful here of the system and make boundary judgments. What is in your control and what would you need to liaise with other members of staff about? Be mindful of your limitations especially regarding time and expertise. Draw on the **interrelationships** you have developed and start gathering information before any decisions or meetings have taken place. Be open and prepared to iterate the approach and ensure that all players in the system know that the approach is iterative.

Step 1: Discuss with the learner and parents the recommendations and prioritise those which you all agree are high priority. This step may be carried out by the SENCo, and they may provide you with the strategies to implement in the classroom.

Step 2: Identify the strategies which need increased commitment and additional work outside the classroom and consider the impact on you or the support staff in your setting. How can this be implemented as smoothly as possible?

Step 3: Consider how many of these strategies could be applied in the classroom in general and which ones are specific to the learner.

Step 4: Outline how you will measure if the strategies are working or not.

Step 5: Create a list of resources which might be needed and whether there will be any additional cost.

Moment of Reflection 8.2: Interrelationships

Consider the flowchart in Figure 8.1 and the feedback loops which might support the process but also limit it.

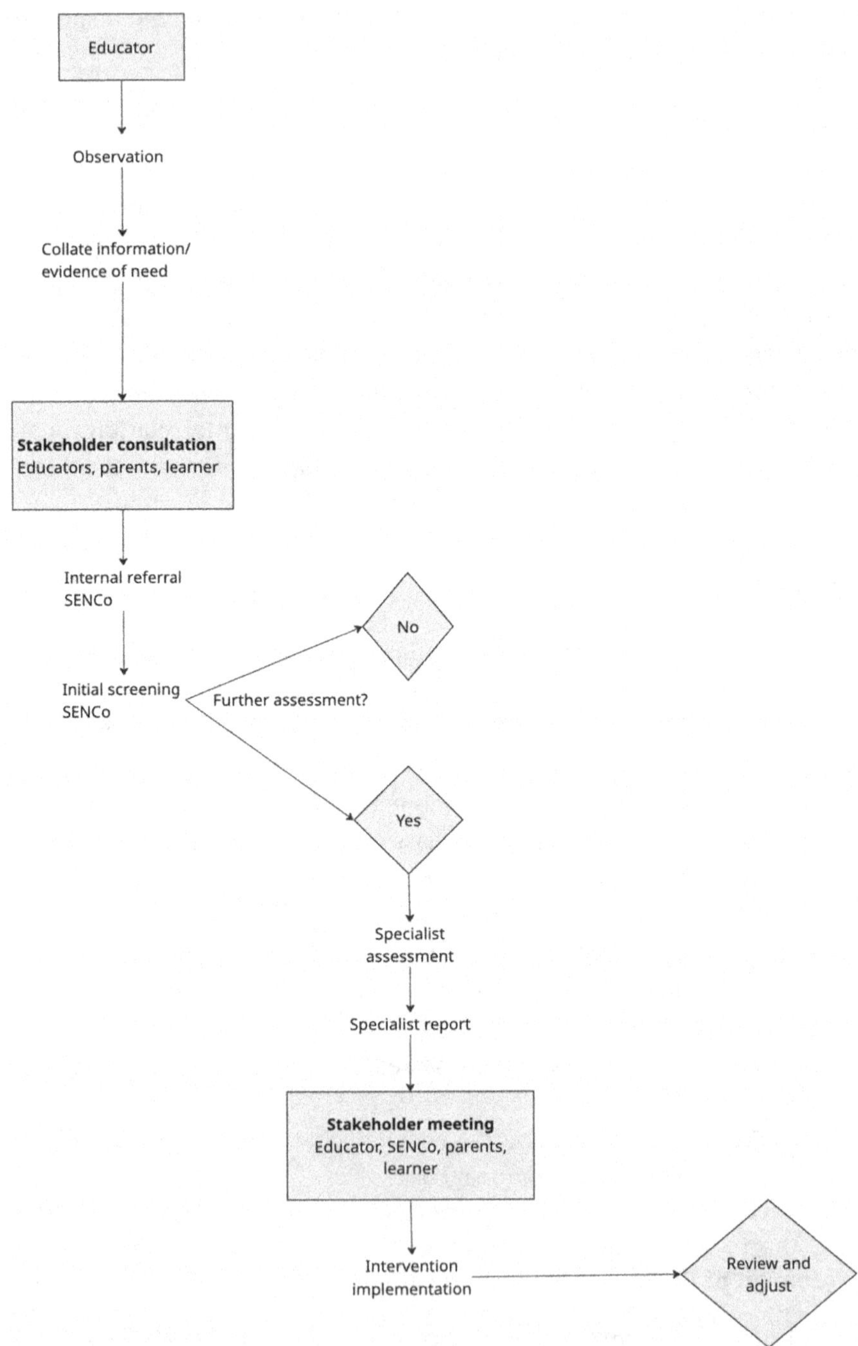

Figure 8.1 A flowchart of referring a learner for further assessment

Consider the referral from the practitioner to the SENCo; how is this done? An online form, face to face? What parameters are set around reporting a need?

How practical is a stakeholder meeting with parents and learners? What could that look like to ensure it achieves its purpose?

What do you do in the time between making a referral for further assessment and receiving recommendations?

Who tracks interventions? Are these targeted to individuals or small groups or a whole school initiative such as Drop Everything and Read?

Identifying a Learner's Normal Way of Working

Practitioners play a crucial role in the initial identification of a learner's needs and when considering putting someone forward for an assessment, a class practitioner may be asked to provide evidence of the learner's normal way of working or more in-depth information on their behaviour and learning. This could be a questionnaire or an online form to gather evidence of that learner's normal way of working. You cannot underestimate the importance of your learner observations and how pivotal the information that you share on the learner is to an assessment of need. Equally, if the evidence that is being gathered is to apply for an Education, Health and Care Plan or for access arrangements, understanding what a learner does day to day is of paramount importance. Especially if the assessor is an outside professional and may only work with a learner for a couple of hours. It is unlikely they would be able to carry out observations of that learner's normal way of working in order to inform the diagnostic decision or any recommendations they make. They will be reliant on the information from the setting to fill in this part of a learner's profile.

Never underestimate what you do every day to meet the needs of your learners. Many of those small changes or tweaks to your plans are interventions and really valuable to not only the learner but also to other teachers they might have.

A referral often begins with a practitioner at an education setting seeing a pattern in a learner's work which does not fit with their general performance at an education setting. For example, it might be a geography practitioner who is surprised at the lack of detail in an essay from a Year 8 learner who always contributes to class and demonstrates their learning when faced with short answer questions. It might be an English practitioner who has noticed that a Year 7 learner is starting to avoid reading out loud in class, and when they do read out loud, they stumble over unfamiliar words and find it hard to predict what they sound like.

It could be a maths practitioner that has noticed that a learner seems to avoid the long wordy questions in exams or a history practitioner who has noticed that one learner does not write as much as you'd expect.

This query might be shared with the SENCo of the education setting, and if they have their own referral process, they might conduct a screener and recommend an educational psychologist or specialist practitioner.

You are likely to come across a range of professional reports in your role as a practitioner; some might have recommendations for classroom practice, whilst others might inform one-to-one intervention only.

The following table outlines typical professionals involved in assessments and the focus of their reports.

All the practitioners are regulated by a membership body (although for specialist teachers this is optional but specialist teachers who hold the assessment practising certificate (APC) are listed on the SASC website (SASC.org.uk)).

A professional report does not stand alone, each professional report which a practitioner receives represents an interconnected web of interactions involving various stakeholders. Each report is not just about the learner but also informs and is shaped within education, medical and family systems. All will explore a learner's background history including birth history, milestones, health and familial relations.

Recommendations provided within professional reports create **feedback loops**. When education settings implement suggested strategies, they alter classroom dynamics and learner responses. Observations from these

Table 8.1 Likely professions to provide education settings with reports

Specialist Teacher Assessors	*Educational Psychologist Report*	*Speech and Language Therapist Report*	*Occupational Therapist Report*	*Clinical Psychologist Report*
May hold an assessor practising certificate and will have experience as a practitioner and completed a level 7 qualification in specific learning difficulties.	Registration with the Health and Care Professions Council (HCPC) and educated to doctorate level.	HCPC Registration Focuses on language development, communication difficulties, and developmental language disorder.	HCPC Registration Assess fine motor skills, handwriting, sensory processing, and coordination (dyspraxia, DCD).	HCPC Registration Comprehensive diagnosis and insights into behaviour, emotional and psychological well-being.
Can diagnose specific learning difficulties related to literacy and numeracy.	Can diagnose a wider range of needs and include professional opinion on social and emotional needs and behaviour	Provides specific language intervention approaches for both one-to-one and the classroom.	Includes classroom environmental adjustments, equipment recommendations and sensory strategies.	Recommendations for behaviour, classroom management strategies.
Can advise on ADHD and dyspraxia in relation to learning.	More suitable for complex, co-occurring cases and those that may lead to an Education, Health and Care Plan.	Often will carry out the support themselves.	Will often carry out the support themselves.	Will often recommend counselling or specialist psychological interventions.
Will report on learning performance rather than emotional or behavioural factors.	Has more choice in relation to diagnostic tests than a specialist practitioner.			

interventions then feedback into future assessments, creating a continuous cycle of adaptation and learning.

Moment of Reflection 8.3: Curiosity

How do changes you implement from a professional report affect classroom dynamics beyond the targeted learner?

What systemic constraints (time, resources, communication) might limit or enable effective use of these professional reports?

Can you identify feedback loops within your classroom interventions suggested by professional reports? How do you track these?

Things to Look Out for When Reading a Report

1. That the author is part of a recognised professional body, such as the SpLD Assessment Standards Committee (SASC) for specialist assessors or the Health and Care Professions Council (HCPC) for health-related roles such as speech and language or occupational therapy.
2. That the report includes standardised scores and there is credible interpretation of these scores.
3. That recommendations are specific to that learner's needs and not a list of generic strategies.
4. That there is an understanding of the learner's environment.
5. That some background history of the learner's early development and education to date has been included.

As an assessor there is an ethical duty to ensure that any testing carried out is as a result of a solid evidence base. A diagnosis can sometimes rely on a background history of difficulties, that support or an intervention has been tried and the difficulties persisted and that there are some areas of cognitive ability which can't be explained for any other reason, including gaps in education, English as an additional language or another specific learning difficulty.

Table 8.2 A brief overview of who can diagnose different learning difficulties

ADHD	*Autism*	*Developmental Language Disorder*
Paediatrician	Paediatrician	Speech and language therapist
Child and adolescent psychiatrist	Child and adolescent psychiatrist	Paediatrician
Specialist ADHD clinic	Clinical psychologist	Clinical or education psychologist
Specialist clinical psychologist	Multidisciplinary team (including speech and language therapists, occupational therapists and psychologists)	Specialist neurodevelopment teams
Dyslexia/Dyscalculia	*Dyspraxia or Developmental Coordination Difficulties*	
Specialist practitioner assessor	Paediatrician	
Educational psychologist	Occupational therapist	
Clinical psychologist	Physiotherapist Neurologist	

Moment of Reflection 8.4: Interrelationships

The majority of these specialists are health care based which will affect the purpose of the assessment and subsequent report. What impact could that have on their recommendations for education?

Targeted and Specialist Support and the Part You Play

An Education, Health and Care Plan (EHCP) is a legal document that sets out the special educational, health and social care needs of a child or young person aged 0–25. It describes the extra help that will be provided to meet those needs and how that help will support the learner or young person to achieve their goals.

EHCPs are for learners and young people who have significant and complex special educational needs (SEN) that cannot be met by the usual support that is available in their setting. This could include children and young people with:

- A physical disability
- A learning difficulty
- A communication difficulty
- A social, emotional or mental health difficulty
- A sensory impairment

The EHC process starts with a referral. This often requires contributions from a team of people, including practitioners, social workers, health professionals and the child or young person's parents or carers. The process will look at the child or young person's needs across all three areas: education, health and social care. It might include several of the professional reports covered earlier in this chapter.

If the assessment finds that the child or young person has significant and complex needs that cannot be met by the usual support that is available, then an EHCP will be written. The EHCP will be shared in draft with the family and other involved parties. If the family disagrees with the final report, they may require mediation or appeal to a SEND tribunal.

The EHCP will set out the child or young person's needs, the support that will be provided to meet those needs and how that support will be delivered. The EHCP will also set out the child or young person's goals and how their progress will be monitored.

EHCPs can be a lifeline for children and young people with significant and complex SEN. They can help to ensure that these children and young people get the support they need to reach their full potential. At the time of writing this book, EHCPs are under review.

Here are some of the benefits of having an EHCP:

- It can help to ensure that a child or young person gets the right support at the right time.
- It can give parents/cares more choice about where their child or young person attends an education setting.
- It can help to improve a child's or young person's educational outcomes.
- It can help to reduce stress and anxiety for parents/carers and their child or young person.

The role you will play in the application for an Education, Health and Care Plan could be minimal or pivotal, but the approach should be the same. This is where the evidence gathering which you have done for those learners that you identified as needing a bit more support either all the time or occasionally is important. It is unlikely that a learner in your class who is going through the process of applying for an EHCP does not already have a history of need and a programme of support including classroom intervention.

Moment of Reflection 8.5: Multiple Perspectives

Review the case study for the following aspects:

1. What would your role be in each step? How would you support the process? Consider the levels of support that might be needed from written evidence to emotional support for the parents and learner.
2. If you are unfamiliar with the EHC process, who could you ask for support or to share their experience? Is this available in your setting? If it is not, is there something you can implement to support future practitioners?
3. How would you manage the potential criticism of the setting and its approach to intervention?
4. How would you support the learner if it is identified that they require a change in provision; again, consider the different levels of support that might be required.

Case Study 5: A Family Applying for an EHCP

Background: Parents with a 9-year-old learner, Sam, who has special educational needs (SEN).

Primary Concern: Sam is autistic and has social communication challenges, which affect academic progress and social integration in school.

Challenges: The current school support is insufficient to meet Sam's complex needs and the parent/school relationship is starting to break down.

Goal: To secure an EHCP for Sam, ensuring access to tailored educational, health and care services.

Key Steps in the EHCP Application Process

Initial Concerns and School Involvement:

- Parents' Observations: Sam exhibits significant challenges in reading, writing and maintaining focus at home, and has difficulty interacting with peers.
- School Support: Sam's school has implemented an individual education plan, but progress is limited, and the school recommends exploring an EHCP.
- Communication with School: The family meets with the Special Educational Needs Coordinator (SENCo) to discuss options for additional support through an EHCP.

Gathering Evidence for the EHCP Application:

Assessments and Reports: The family gathers evidence from multiple sources, including:

- School Reports: Documentation of Sam's progress (or lack thereof) under the current support strategies.
- Medical Reports: Sam's diagnosis from a paediatrician, including details on learning, speech and language difficulties.
- Educational Psychologist Report: An external assessment highlighting Sam's specific learning needs and recommendations for support.
- Speech and Language Therapy (SALT) Report: Documentation of Sam's social communication challenges and recommendations for speech therapy.

Parental Request for an EHCP Needs Assessment:

- Formal Application: The parents submit a request for an EHCP assessment to the local authority (LA), outlining Sam's educational, health and care needs.
- School's Support: The school provides written input supporting the application, citing Sam's lack of progress despite the existing interventions.

LA Decision and Needs Assessment:

- Decision Process: The LA reviews the request, evidence and assessments provided by both the family and the school. After consideration, the LA agrees to conduct a full needs assessment.
- Multidisciplinary Involvement: Various professionals (e.g., educational psychologist, speech therapist, SENCo) conduct further assessments to understand Sam's needs comprehensively.

Drafting the EHCP:

Collaboration: The family works with the LA, school and involved professionals to draft the EHCP. This document outlines:

- Sam's Educational Needs: Specific learning difficulties and social communication issues.
- Desired Outcomes: Academic, social and health-related goals for Sam (e.g., improved reading and communication skills, better social integration).
- Support Plan: A detailed plan of the support Sam requires, including one-on-one teaching assistants, specialised educational resources and speech therapy sessions.

Review and Finalisation:

- Parental Input: The parents review the draft EHCP and suggest amendments based on their understanding of Sam's needs.
- Final EHCP: After feedback and adjustments, the LA finalises the EHCP, which becomes a legally binding document.
- Named School: The EHCP specifies the type of school Sam should attend to meet their needs, whether mainstream with additional support or a special educational setting.

Ongoing Monitoring and Review:

- Annual Review: The EHCP is subject to annual reviews to ensure that Sam is making progress toward the specified goals and that the support provided remains adequate.
- Adjustments as Needed: As Sam grows and their needs evolve, the family and professionals work together to make necessary changes to the EHCP.

Key Challenges and Resolutions

Navigating the Application Process:

- Challenge: The family initially felt overwhelmed by the complexity of the application process and the volume of evidence required.
- Resolution: With support from the SENCo and external professionals, the family received guidance on gathering the necessary documentation and submitting a well-prepared application.

Ensuring the EHCP Reflected Sam's Full Needs:

- Challenge: Initial drafts of the EHCP did not fully address Sam's social and emotional needs, focusing mainly on academic challenges.
- Resolution: The family advocated for adjustments, ensuring that goals related to Sam's emotional well-being and social skills were included.

Outcomes

Tailored Support in Place:

- Sam now receives one-on-one support from a teaching assistant, as well as access to specialist services such as speech and language therapy and occupational therapy.
- Specific accommodations in the classroom, such as modified teaching materials and reduced workload, help Sam engage more effectively with the curriculum.

Improved Academic and Social Progress:

- Since the EHCP was implemented, Sam has shown marked improvement in literacy and communication skills. The personalised support has enabled Sam to keep pace with learning objectives.
- Socially, Sam has developed stronger relationships with peers, supported by structured social skill-building interventions.

Parental Confidence:

- The parents feel empowered by the support and are more confident that Sam's needs are being adequately addressed, both academically and emotionally.

Legal Protections:

- With the EHCP in place, Sam's support is legally protected, ensuring the family has recourse if the school or LA fails to provide the necessary services.

Moment of Reflection 8.6: Interrelationships

Consider the outcomes from this EHCP and the introduction of a one-to-one teaching assistant.

How would this work in your classroom? Is there room for another body in your classroom? What is the class set-up and will it need to be reviewed in order to accommodate this additional person?

How will the dynamics of the classroom change and what can you do to prepare for this?

What can you do to work with this new person and ensure they are happy and feel welcome in your classroom?

As a result of Sam's EHCP what do you know you need to consider in regard to your planning? How might this impact your VSM (systems 1, 2 and 3)?

As a practitioner, you are often the first person to notice when something is not quite working for a learner. You are not expected to hold all the answers or know what to do right away and it is not possible to meet the needs of every learner without support at times.

Moment of Reflection 8.7: Curiosity

Consider one of your classes and identify how many have a formal diagnosis, are known to the SENCo and receive pupil premium, and how many do you support with their learning but do not have a diagnosis. Do you tailor your planning to the needs of your cohort, or do you meet the needs of individuals? How many learners with individual needs does it take to become the majority?

Some learners will always need more targeted support, and others will require it for set periods of time. When that happens, the practitioners become part of a much wider system and further reflection on the change in role/dynamics is required.

This chapter explored how to make sense of that wider system, how to work with professional recommendations, and how to keep the learner's day-to-day experience at the heart of every choice made to support them. It's a balancing act between systematic constraints and individual needs and at times this can be frustrating. But maintaining an open and curious approach to support and ensuring that the learner's voice is included in any decision made will ground your practice in inclusion.

Moments of Reflection

- 8.1 Practice
- 8.2 Interrelationships
- 8.3 Curiosity
- 8.4 Interrelationships
- 8.5 Multiple Perspectives
- 8.6 Interrelationships
- 8.7 Curiosity

9

Mind Health and Its Impact on Learning

Overview

Whilst this chapter addresses some aspects of mind health, its intention is to outline some of the behaviours and contributing factors to challenges with learning. Clinical language such as depression and anxiety needs to be treated with care, and therefore the letters from Jo Robinson, a trained counsellor, will use these terms but otherwise 'worry/apprehension', 'low mood' and 'stress' will be used in this chapter as I am not a trained mental health practitioner. The intention is to ensure that the focus is on mind health and promoting healthy emotional awareness.

It is important to note that any concerns regarding someone's mind health, especially that of children and young people, should not be overlooked or minimised but discussed with the safeguarding lead in your setting. Whilst the strategies outlined in this chapter support classroom-based intervention, if difficulties persist or become more pervasive, they must be reported.

Consider the VSM model introduced in Chapter 2. If one of the communication channels is dominated by worry or intrusive thoughts, it will be difficult for any productive work to be done. It will make the first system sluggish, and the work will soon start to pile up.

It is also important to reflect upon the perception of mental health in your setting and consider it right through each system in the VSM.

- **System 5 Governance**

What policies are there for mind health, what terminology is used? Are there separate policies for learners and staff? Is it the same

DOI: 10.4324/9781003400639-10

terminology or different? If it's different, why? How does that affect the culture of the school?

- **System 4 Opportunities and Threats**

What from system 5 provides opportunities to explore mind health; what might have a negative impact?

What is required to inform your planning?

Are there opportunities to inform both best practice and policy?

- **System 3 Planning and Organisation**

How do you plan and monitor the mind health of your learners? What about your own mind health? How do you factor in healthy practices for your own mind health?

- **System 2 Communication**

How is mind health monitored both explicitly and implicitly?
What communication channels exist? Consider what is in place for communicating concern, such as self-reporting or reporting anonymously.

- **System 1 Operations**

Do you make space in your practice to discuss mind health? What does that look like?

How is it monitored? What preparation do you give learners before discussing sensitive topics? Is it subject related?

Moment of Reflection 9.1: Curiosity

You have built a wealth of knowledge through this book and the recommendations in the list above are reflective questions relating mind health to the VSM. Before you read on, address these questions.

Stress in the Context of the School Calendar

Stress is necessary in order to get things done and a certain level of stress is healthy. It can support productivity, ambition and in turn lead to feelings of accomplishment and boost self-confidence. However, too much stress can lead to burnout, shutdown or overwhelm. What stress feels like for an individual can be difficult to understand and sometimes difficult to dissociate from other similar feelings which might be related to hormones, emotions or learning difficulties.

Stress is also something which can increase at certain times in the year.

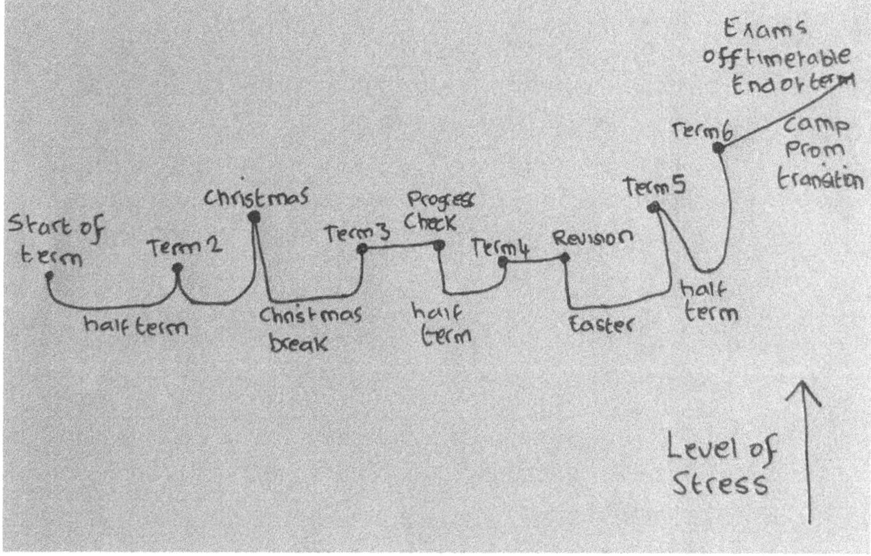

Figure 9.1 The highs and lows of stressful moments during a school year

Moment of Reflection 9.2: Multiple Perspectives

Consider the following times in a school's calendar and rank them from most to least stressful for a learner.

1. The first day of school
2. Sports day
3. Christmas
4. Exams

5. Last day of school
6. Prom or out-of-school-hours social events
7. Camp or outings
8. Cover lessons

Your hierarchy is likely to be similar for all learners but for those with additional learning needs, the difference will be that the feelings of stress may take longer to reduce, and they may need support to deal with this.

The first and most important thing to acknowledge is the change in routine and not to minimise any feelings of stress or anxiety.

Furthermore, work with the learner to identify ways to support them through this time and share information with other practitioners to make the next occasion a little smoother again.

Repeating this with learners will help to inform your practice and prepare for perceived stressful times and hopefully reduce stress for the learners.

As mentioned, some stress is good but if a learner begins to demonstrate the following behaviours frequently, it might be important to address what is making them feel so stressed:

- Increased irritability
- Mood swings
- Withdrawal from classroom activities
- Difficulty staying on task
- Increased absence
- Physical symptoms such as headaches, fatigue, stomach aches
- Over-dependence on the practitioner/teaching assistant or peers

Moment of Reflection 9.3: Curiosity

Take some time to consider your own stress levels and if you relate to any of the points above; be kind to yourself, and if you need to, share any concerns you have about your own stress with your line manager or if you have access, the school counsellor. There are also several organisations set up to support teachers and their mental wellness which can be searched for online.

Worries and Anxiety

Worry and anxiety is something we all have but when it takes hold, it can debilitate and dictate life choices in a way which feels out of the person's control. It can disrupt learning, friendships, home life and can, over time, erode a person's identity and autonomy.

If the ultimate goal is to ensure that what is taught is accessible, it is imperative that mind health is part of the system. Worry and anxiety have been included for the following reasons but it is recognised that they can be part of other mind health challenges which are equally as valid:

1. The increase in anxiety-related issues in schools (BBC, 2025)
2. The impact that worry/anxiety can have on working memory and processing (see Chapter 5)
3. The co-occurrence of anxiety with other specific learning difficulties

Anxiety and worry is not contained, it does not happen only at particular times of the day or in certain situations. It can manifest in different ways and may be more noticeable at various times. Learners may be able to manage these feelings in school, but at home, where they feel safe, the emotions are released which leads to tension and concern at home.

Moment of Reflection 9.4: Practice

Take some time to consider what behaviours you might have seen which could have been as a result of worry and what you could do to reduce these worries.

The following letter is from Jo Robinson, an experienced counsellor who has worked with a range of individuals and shares her insights into what practitioners firstly need to be aware of and secondly what they can do to support the individual without overstepping the boundaries of being a practitioner and not a counsellor.

Dear practitioner,

The different faces of anxiety

As a counsellor who works with learners and young people in schools and in private practice, I have seen countless young clients come through the doors whose anxiety is getting in the way of achieving their full potential in education. According to Anxiety UK, 17% (1 in 6) 6- to 16-year-olds experience one or more mental disorders, and in 2023 the counselling organisation Place2Be claimed that 78% of young people seen by one of their counsellors have 'experienced anxiety in a social setting'. It's safe to say that anxiety is present in all my clients to a varying degree – and it has many different faces.

What is anxiety and what does it look like in education?

Anxiety is a normal physiological response to a stressful situation. We all experience anxiety at some stage in our lives, as it helps us to deal with adverse events. However, when our stress response outlasts the situation, becomes overwhelming, interferes with our ability to carry out daily tasks, or there is no obvious situation causing the feeling, anxiety can be a problem.

Schools and places of education are hugely important to a learner's development and form a large part of their emerging sense of self. They have a bigger impact on their growth and mental health than we give credit for. Even the smallest of actions by practitioners and peers can have a lasting impact on how a young person experiences the world and, ultimately, how they respond to it. In a post-COVID era, where vital skills such as socialisation, self-regulation and communication have suffered and mental health has been impacted (NSPCC Learning, 2022), recognising and managing anxiety in schools has become more important than ever.

Recognising anxiety

Anxiety does not always appear as we would expect. A loud, disruptive, defiant learner may feel equally as anxious on the inside as one who is quiet and reserved and who avoids speaking up in lessons. Some learners are adept at communicating how they feel, others are not. One young person may act out their anxiety with disruptive behaviours and bullying, another will avoid school completely. Poor concentration, panic attacks, OCD behaviours, phobias and self-harm can also be signs that anxiety is bubbling underneath.

When a learner's anxiety increases, their ability to perform other skills is negatively affected. This includes working memory (the ability to hold and retrieve information), self-regulation (managing difficult feelings and adapting behaviourally), executive functioning skills (envisaging future goals and taking steps to achieve them) and accurate thinking. Anxiety often leads to negative thinking such as catastrophising (assuming the worst will happen) and all or nothing thinking ('I am awful at Maths!', rather than 'I am just finding algebra tricky'). As a result, learners suffering with anxiety are pulled into a negative cycle: poor executive functioning skills cause anxiety in school, which in turn causes poor executive functioning and inaccurate thinking, which then leads to disengagement.

How can we help a learner who is struggling with anxiety?

Helping anxious learners is as much about creating the right environment as it is about stepping in with strategies. Safety is key, and this comes in different packages, but the physical space you create and the relationship you forge with learners should be central. Having structured routines and clear instructions will also decrease anxiety around uncertainty.

Above all, acknowledging anxiety and validating a learner's feelings are vital, even if it seems they are overreacting. Providing a safe space for them to talk that is non-judgemental should be priority. There can be many different causes and contributors to anxiety; sometimes it will be easy to get to the bottom of, but it's common for learners and young people not to know why they feel anxious. If there are complicated underlying reasons for the anxiety, or if it is particularly severe, therapy may be the best option. In other cases, there are things that can help in the classroom. Either way, creating the right environment, validating their feelings and incorporating strategies in the classroom are key.

So, remember the top five tips:

1. *Cultivate a safe and calming classroom environment.*
2. *Build positive relationships.*
3. *Have structured routines.*
4. *Incorporate and model coping strategies.*
5. *Validate feelings.*

Taking care of yourself

Remember – you will also have a relationship with anxiety, so it's important to reflect on your own experience of the feeling, and how you manage it. I encourage you to spend some time reflecting on what anxiety means for you, how you take care of yourself, and ask yourself if you are doing enough of it? Visit Anxiety UK for some useful tools for self-care.

After all, you can't look after others without looking after yourself first.

Jo Robinson

MBACP

BA(Hons), PG(Dip), PG(DipSup)

Maintaining Routine and Consistency to Mitigate Worries

Whilst the feelings of an anxious learner should be acknowledged and not belittled, strategies to support progress should be prioritised. The more a learner is withdrawn from a classroom, the harder it is for them to return. One tip to achieve this is to focus on the future rather than delving into the

Figure 9.2 A calm classroom

past and signposting the individual to counselling services in order for them to deal with the underlying issues of their mind health challenges.

Other strategies to manage worry in the classroom are:

- Keep them busy and engaged in an activity.
- Suggest they complete a task around the classroom, for example handing out the books or tidying a cupboard.
- Give them a specific time to complete the task and set high expectations for them to return to the work set.
- If they struggle to silence their inner voice and you are unable to give them time, there and then to talk, ensure you give them some time at the end of the session. Again, use a timer to limit the conversation but when you offer the time, give it without distraction.

The speed at which information is consumed combined with dopamine-inducing scrolling on social media is likely to have had an effect on society's ability to concentrate. It is important to refer back to working memory and remember the capacity for information in children and young people and how this is still developing. Whilst their neuroreceptors and capacity for taking on new information are in their prime, there are other factors which will reduce this capacity and are very much out of their hands. Think hormonal changes, risk-taking urges and the development of identity. Particularly in teenagers, these drives will all be in competition for their attention.

Consider this vicious cycle of digital consumption and the effect it can have on the necessary cognitive skills required for learning.

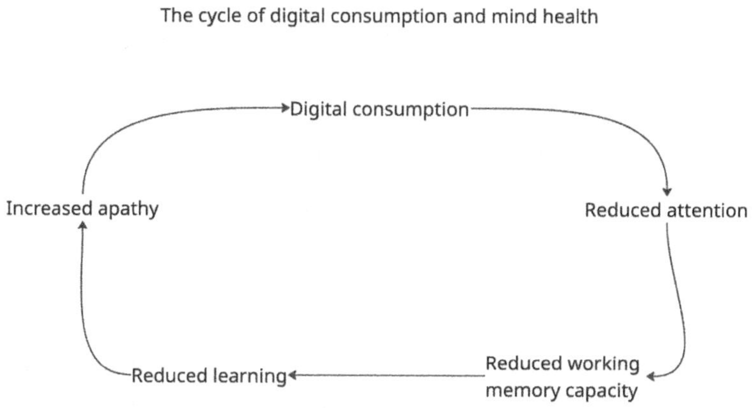

Figure 9.3 A causal loop of digital viewing and mind health

Moment of Reflection 9.5: Curiosity

Where are the leverage points in this diagram that you could influence?

Some ideas include teaching mindfulness techniques to support focus, providing guidance on self-regulation and providing engaging, scaffolded tasks which increase a learner's stamina for study.

In Chapter 5, the importance of processing and working memory was considered for the acquisition of learning. Worries and anxiety can impede both of these cognitive functions in several ways.

1. Intrusive Thoughts

When your mind is racing with other thoughts it can be difficult to establish the focus needed to take on new information. It is as if your brain has used up all its space for information and there is no more capacity left. The information whether it is being delivered by a practitioner or through a text remains known on a surface level only. The capacity to connect with the information on a deeper level, which is necessary for retention, is slim when there is little space for it.

2. Imposter Syndrome

If you have any doubt about your ability, there will be little capacity to take risks, and therefore you are unlikely to put yourself forward to answer questions or take the lead role in group work. You are unlikely to want to explore ideas for fear of getting it wrong and you will therefore become a passive member of the class.

3. Exhaustion

Each one of these examples leads to the person being passive and they might have the best of intentions to do well in the subject, but it is unlikely they will unless they have some strategies to mitigate all the above.

4. Maintaining Focus

As mentioned earlier, with increased time on digital devices which is not only for recreation but also for learning, the time spent reading text or referring to books is now limited. In contrast to this is a continued reliance on recording information by writing it and examinations remaining on paper. There is a disconnect between how our brains are being moulded to receive information and what happens in a classroom.

Many schools are taking action such as banning phones in schools which creates conditions for learning that hopefully support better focus and attention.

Moment of Reflection 9.6: Curiosity

Recognising, supporting and talking about mind health can be challenging. Step back into your reflective mode and consider your worldview of mind health and your own knowledge and experience. How does this impact your practice? What influence does it have?

What practices do you include in the classroom to support mind health?

The case study below could also be relevant for other learners who find regularly attending school a challenge, as whilst it features a learner with anxiety, the outcome of non-attendance is not specifically related to anxiety.

As you read this, there will be call-outs throughout which will remind you of the viable systems model, interrelationships and multiple perspectives.

Case Study 6: A 14-Year-Old with Anxiety Struggling to Attend School

Background: 14-year-old experiencing diagnosed anxiety, making regular school attendance difficult.

Primary Challenge: Severe anxiety, especially around school, leading to frequent absenteeism and difficulty keeping up with academic and social demands.

Behaviours: Panic attacks, overwhelming fear of school environments, low self-esteem, avoidance behaviours (e.g., staying home), and falling behind in academics.

Impact: Reduced academic performance, social isolation and emotional distress.

Identified Challenges and System Components

Anxiety Triggers:

1. School Environment: Loud classrooms, crowded hallways, pressure to perform, and social interactions are overwhelming.
2. Fear of Judgement: Fear of being judged by peers or practitioners, and anxiety about academic failure.
3. Panic Attacks: Heightened physical symptoms (e.g., rapid heartbeat, nausea) during the thought or anticipation of attending school.

Moment of Reflection 9.7: Interrelationships

VSM System 1: You have already carried out a classroom audit of extraneous variables (Chapter 5). Apply this to the whole school and evaluate the possible causes of overwhelm in your setting.

Key Stakeholders:

- Parents: Provide emotional support but are also concerned about the learner falling behind in school.
- School Staff: Teaching staff, school counsellors, learner support are trying to help the learner but finding it difficult to accommodate the level of absenteeism. They fear she is falling behind but they also have pressures from national standards to ensure that learners attend school.
- Mental Health Professional: A therapist or counsellor working with the learner on managing anxiety through cognitive-behavioural therapy (CBT) and other strategies.
- Peers: Limited interaction with friends at school due to frequent absences, leading to feelings of social isolation.

Moment of Reflection 9.8: Multiple Perspectives

Review the stakeholder map completed in Chapter 1. Who is the key player regarding supporting mind health? How could you improve communication between the stakeholders in this situation?

System Mapping (Factors Influencing Anxiety and School Attendance):

These are all causal loops and the importance of identifying such feedback loops is then working on how to interrupt them.

- Anxiety ↔ School Attendance: Higher anxiety leads to lower attendance, which increases academic pressure and worsens anxiety.
- Social Isolation ↔ Anxiety: Social isolation from peers worsens the learner's anxiety, making it harder to reintegrate into the school environment.
- Academic Pressure ↔ Avoidance: The more the learner falls behind academically, the more anxious they feel about returning to school, perpetuating a cycle of avoidance.

Immediate Challenges:

- Increased Absenteeism: The learner misses several days of school each week, falling behind in classwork.
- Negative Self-Image: The learner feels incapable of managing their anxiety, leading to a loss of confidence and self-worth.
- Parental Concern: Parents are unsure how to best support their learner, balancing their mind health needs with the need to maintain an education.

Systems Thinking Approach to Intervention

Identifying Key Leverage Points:

- Mental Health Support: Prioritising the role of therapy and counselling to help the learner develop coping mechanisms for anxiety. Liaise with the parents and get private support if they have the resources. Signpost them to charities which offer free counselling for young people. Speak with their GP for a referral to mind health support services.

- Flexible School Attendance: Implementing a gradual return to school with partial days or specific classes to reduce the overwhelming nature of the full school day.
- Home Learning Support: Providing access to online learning tools or homework assignments to stay connected to school while managing anxiety at home.
- Creating Safe Spaces at School: Establishing a safe, quiet area within the school where the learner can go if feeling overwhelmed.
- Provide a Key Worker: This might be their tutor or class practitioner or another trusted adult. Confer with the learner to find out who their go-to person is as it might not be who you expect.

Developing Strategies:

- Cognitive Behavioural Therapy (CBT; NHS, 2025): Working with a therapist to challenge negative thoughts about school and develop healthier coping mechanisms.
- Exposure Therapy: Gradually increasing exposure to the school environment by attending one class per day, slowly building up to full days over time.
- Supportive Conversations: Regular check-ins with parents and school staff to ensure the learner feels supported and heard.
- Mindfulness and Relaxation Techniques: Introducing breathing exercises, mindfulness, and relaxation strategies to manage anxiety before and during school.

Moment of Reflection 9.9: Boundary Judgement

Which of the suggested resources are within your remit to resource? Which would require additional funding and how could that be achieved?

Modifying the School System:

- Alternative Education Options: Exploring part-time schooling, homeschooling, or hybrid models to accommodate the learner's mind health needs while still pursuing education.

- School Counsellor Involvement: Weekly meetings with the school counsellor to provide a safe outlet for discussing anxiety and school-related concerns.
- Practitioner Collaboration: Practitioners being aware of the learner's situation and adapting expectations (e.g., reduced homework load, extended deadlines) to reduce pressure.

Addressing Feedback Loops:

- Avoidance ↔ Anxiety Cycle: Breaking the cycle of avoidance by creating positive experiences in the school environment and celebrating small successes (e.g., attending one class without panic).
- Academic Progress ↔ Confidence: As the learner makes progress academically through small steps (e.g., completing assignments at home), their confidence improves, helping reduce overall anxiety.
- Parental Support ↔ Learner Confidence: Parents using positive reinforcement and understanding reduces pressure on the learner, which helps them approach school more positively.

Outcomes of the Systems Thinking Approach

Gradual Reintegration into School:

- The learner starts attending school for limited periods, beginning with a few classes and slowly increasing their attendance over several weeks.
- The safe space at school and accommodations help reduce feelings of overwhelm.

Improved Mind Health:

- Regular therapy and counselling provide the learner with coping mechanisms, resulting in fewer panic attacks and better management of their anxiety.
- The learner begins practicing mindfulness techniques to manage in-the-moment anxiety.

Academic Stabilisation:

- Online resources and home learning reduce academic pressure, allowing the learner to keep up with lessons despite limited school attendance.
- Practitioners provide tailored support, and assignments are broken down into manageable tasks, reducing the stress of falling behind.

Improved Social Engagement:

As anxiety is managed, the learner starts reconnecting with peers through online communication and group activities at school, reducing feelings of isolation.

Reflection

- Holistic Approach: By addressing both the academic and emotional needs of the learner, the systems thinking approach provides a balanced solution to reintegrate the learner into school life.
- Long-Term Support: While challenges remain, the learner is learning lifelong skills in managing anxiety, and the gradual reintegration into school is helping rebuild their self-esteem.
- Collaborative Effort: The cooperation between parents, school staff and mental health professionals ensures that the learner feels supported and empowered.

Low Mood and Depression

Depression has been on the increase in learners with an increase from 15% of young people in 2010 to 41% in 2021 (Statista, 2022).

Much like worry, low mood can be exacerbated by the trappings of modern life such as time on screens and social media, although it must also be acknowledged that some young people can seek both solace and support in their online community.

It is important to be open minded when discussing a learner's habits and not be dismissive about the way they spend their leisure time. However, spending lots of time isolated and in their rooms can be an indicator of low mood, and when combined with some of the behaviours below may call for further investigation, depending on their age and the school setting.

Depression is often associated with low mood but can also include the following behaviours:

- Persistent sadness
- Tearfulness
- Feelings of hopelessness or guilt
- Irritability, anger or hostility
- Difficulty in making decisions
- Decline in academic performance
- Risk taking behaviours
- Increased dependence on caregivers or friends
- Or the opposite, withdrawing from others or secretive behaviour
- Loss of appetite
- Weight loss or weight gain
- Low energy/fatigue
- Increased sensitivity to criticism or being told off

In the classroom you may want to avoid asking them to contribute to discussions as they may lack confidence in their ideas or not wish to be called out.

Homework tasks are likely to take them longer if they are experiencing bouts of lethargy and they may find it hard to think of ideas for timed pieces in school. Providing them with the option to bullet point their ideas can get them going; maybe allow them to embellish their writing on another day.

You might notice that the learner is not attending so regularly, and having low-threat, consistent strategies to support this will help them to not fall behind. Providing online notes and access to shared documents will help them to access the work at home if necessary.

Moment of Reflection 9.10: Curiosity

Consider your level of knowledge regarding mind health? Are there any areas which you might need to know more about? Who can you ask in your setting regarding training? What whole school directives are there for supporting mind health?

Practitioners should avoid highlighting any absences upon a learner's return and check-ins with the learner should be carried out discreetly.

If the VSM is considered, in particular system 2 (the methods of communication) and system 1 (the nuts and bolts of the classroom), is there anything additional which would need adding here to support learners with mind health challenges?

- Would a shared notes board be a useful addition to your online resources?
- Could this support those who missed education due to mind health challenges?
- Can you develop a bare minimum curriculum for those learners who miss a lot of education to the point where catching up might not be possible, but they could still sit examinations and pass?

Feelings of anxiety and low mood are a common experience, however for learners, these feelings can be new and scary especially if they have physical symptoms. Therefore, they need more support in firstly understanding those feelings and subsequently dealing with them. No matter how big or small these feelings are, knowing that someone is listening and is there for them, even if it might not be possible to completely understand what they are going through, can empower learners to make progress.

The patchwork of needs can include neurodiversity, poverty, mind health challenges and social or familial challenges, and it is important to be flexible, curious and non-judgemental in these situations and not consider one need as greater or more important than another.

Moment of Reflection 9.11: Practice

When reading through Jo's letter about depression reflect upon the three areas highlighted by Jo: mood, thinking and activity.

Mood: How can you ensure your language and the way you communicate with the learners instils positivity and compassion?

Thinking: How can you scaffold thinking time to ensure it is productive and not too open ended to allow time for negative thoughts?

Activity: Reflect on your choice of activities and how inclusive they are for learners with mind health challenges.

Jo Robinson, having explained anxiety from her professional perspective, is here again to outline depression and how to support learners in the classroom.

Dear practitioner,

Depression in the classroom

Following on from my letter about anxiety, I would like to talk a little about my experience of counselling children and young people with depression.

The terms 'depression and anxiety' are often used together, and it is common for them both to be present in people who are struggling with their mental health. The symptoms can overlap and both depression and anxiety commonly occur alongside other conditions such as autism and ADHD. This means that we see them a lot, in one form or another, in and outside of education.

However, it is important not to lump together the two conditions, as we can run the risk of missing an opportunity to make a difference in the life of a sufferer. Recent research shows that treatment, which is typically the same for both depression and anxiety, is less effective for depression than it is for anxiety (Weisz, 2024).

This is why it is important to consider depression on its individual attributes, as a condition that, independently of anything else, has a deep impact on its sufferers and those around them.

What is depression?

The World Health Organisation estimates that depression occurs in 1.4% of adolescents aged 10–14 years, and 3.5% of 15–19-year-olds, and is more prevalent in girls. On average, an episode of depression in a child or adolescent lasts for about eight months and 70% of those whose depression eases will develop another depressive episode within the next five years (Birmaher et al., 2007).

The causes of depression in children and young people are often complex and tend to include a combination of environmental and genetic factors. Symptoms include feeling consistently low, sad or flat, every day, for a period of a few weeks or more, along with a diminished ability to manage fluctuating emotions. It affects three main areas – mood, thinking and activity – decreases motivation, increases irritability and reduces the ability to experience joy. It is more than just a response to a difficult event (for example feeling low for a few days after a fall-out with a friend); it is an acute and chronic problem.

In terms of neurobiology, depression shrinks brain volume in the hippocampus and cortical regions. The condition negatively impacts growth and development, school performance, peer or family relationships and can lead to self-harm and suicide. It is not something to be taken lightly.

How can you spot depression in children and young people?

Unlike anxiety, where symptoms can present externally and be easier to spot, depression is more about what's happening on the inside. Adolescents have often described feelings of worthlessness and self-criticism, finding their focus and concentration skills are decreasing. In younger children, physical symptoms such as tummy aches and unexplained pains tend to be more prominent (NICE, 2005).

In the classroom, anxious kids might be easier to spot as they are quick to engage and eager to learn. Conversely, depression saps energy and motivation, and learners struggling with low mood will find it harder to connect, tougher to engage and might even lack the motivation to attend school altogether.

What is depression telling us?

Having worked with children and young people for nearly a decade in both school counselling services and private practice, I see depression as a symptom of a wider problem. It's telling us something about a bigger picture that children and young people are struggling to verbalise.

There are two important aspects to consider when we think about what depression could be telling us:

1. ***Common environmental causes***

In addition to genetic predisposition, depression can be triggered by environmental causes. These can include poverty, negative family relationships, parental divorce, bullying, school/exam stress and child neglect and abuse. Social media and societal expectations mean that even in primary school children can feel huge pressure to succeed academically and see academic success as directly linked to their worth as a person. Perhaps with the exception of bullying, these are circumstances that are difficult for us to change. A child or young person is very much at the mercy of their environment and lacks the autonomy or resources to change external factors.

2. *Depression is an internalising of feelings and events*

Health professionals refer to depression and anxiety as 'internalising conditions' because they represent problems and feelings that the child has internalised and taken on as their own, rather than acted out through challenging behaviour.

Depression is a sign that a young person is struggling to know where to put their difficult feelings. As mentioned above, a period of depression can be a symptom of a situation that is outside of someone's control.

For example, a child or young person might blame themselves for their parent's break up, or internally carry the sadness of their family. They might turn on themselves if they are being bullied, or feel useless and not know how to help if their family is struggling financially.

What practitioners can do to help

We can't fix the problem of depression. But we can begin to build a different future for our young people by creating an accepting, educational environment that allows a child or young person to better manage their emotions.

We often try to separate educational settings from a child or young person's personal lives and experiences. In my opinion it does not work this way. We have to see the child as a whole - what they experience in the home they bring to school, and what they experience at school they take home - we are all whole, integrated beings.

Most of the following will already be a part of your professional practices, but I want to remind you of their importance:

Prevention

Encourage an environment of talking and acceptance - talk about mental health in the classroom - de-stigmatise mental health problems with open, clear, accessible information. Young Minds has lots of resources that help people to talk about mental health in the classroom.

Being outdoors stimulates brain growth, and movement helps to shift emotions. Encourage outdoor activities, exercise and time in nature. Take lessons outside if you can incorporate movement into the classroom.

Professional help

Support sufferers to access professional therapies - talking about underlying issues will help them to express how they feel in a safe space.

Communication

Build a team around the child and make a plan. Liaise with parents/carers, clinicians and mental health workers to formulate a clear plan to make learning accessible. Include the child and build a plan that is tailored to them; use what works for the individuals.

Model resilience

Teach them about what it means to fail; failure can be as much a positive experience as a negative one. Help them to build their resources to succeed at tasks, not just how to gain a high grade in their final exams.

Celebrate the small things

Try to remain tolerant of what appear to be unsociable moods. With depression comes lack of motivation and unwillingness to engage. Remember that this is not something they can control, and it is not laziness. It is a struggle for depression sufferers to get up in the morning, so celebrate the small successes like making it to school, submitting homework or managing a PE session.

Don't give up on them

Where depression makes it hard for the sufferer to keep going, it also makes it challenging for supporters to continue to cheer them on. Above all else, model your willingness to keep trying. Be a consistent, positive presence in their lives, even when it feels like there is little you can do to help. This will help them to see that even when things are hard, those around them are not giving up on them. It might just be enough to help them see that they shouldn't give up on themselves.

Jo Robinson

MBACP

BA(Hons), PG(Dip), PG(DipSup)

Supporting mind health within a complex system such as education requires compassion and empathy. Recognising and addressing anxiety, stress and depression in learners – and indeed practitioners – is crucial for academic success and long-term well-being.

Considering mind health in relation to a broader system of support such as the suggested VSM ensures complexity and interrelationships are considered and reflected upon. Embedding mindful and chosen practices into daily routines, providing structured support systems and creating environments that validate and respond compassionately to a learner's mind health challenges will underpin a positive and kind approach.

Moreover, it is essential to maintain curiosity and reflective practice, appreciating how dynamic and changeable mind health can be and to know when you as the practitioner might need outside support and to engage stakeholders in meeting the needs of the learner.

The theme of addressing differences through consistent practices rather than when a need arises includes mind health, and creating a supportive culture for everyone will enable progress for all.

Moments of Reflection

- 9.1 Curiosity
- 9.2 Multiple Perspectives
- 9.3 Curiosity
- 9.4 Practice
- 9.5 Curiosity
- 9.6 Curiosity
- 9.7 Interrelationships
- 9.8 Multiple Perspectives
- 9.9 Boundary Judgement
- 9.10 Curiosity
- 9.11 Practice

References

Birmaher, B. et al. (2007). Practice parameter for the assessment and treatment of children and adolescents with depressive disorders. *Journal of the American Academy of Child and Adolescent Psychiatry, 46*(11), 1503–1526. https://pubmed.ncbi.nlm.nih.gov/18049300

National Institute for Health and Clinical Excellence (NICE). (2005). *Depression in children and young people: identification and management in primary, community and secondary care*. NICE Clinical guidelines CG28. www.ncbi.nlm.nih.gov/books/NBK56425

NHS. (2025). Cognitive behavioural therapy (CBT). www.nhs.uk/mental-health/talking-therapies-medicine-treatments/talking-therapies-and-counselling/cognitive-behavioural-therapy-cbt

NSPCC Learning. (2022). *The impact of coronavirus (COVID-19): Statistics briefing*. NSPCC. https://learning.nspcc.org.uk/research-resources/statistics-briefings/covid

Statista. (2022). Share of young people who reported experiences of depression/feeling down in the United Kingdom (UK) from 2009 to 2021. www.statista.com/statistics/1199302/depression-among-young-people-in-the-united-kingdom

Weisz, J. R. (2024). The internalizing paradox-youth anxiety and depression symptoms. *Papers Podcast*. Association for Child and Adolescent Mental Health. https://acamhlearn.org/Learning/The_Internalizing_Paradox_%e2%80%93_Youth_Anxiety_and_Depression_Symptoms/ba40bcbb-4355-4340-bbe4-0c752719f059

10
One Change at a Time . . .

Dear practitioner,

As the book draws to a close, I have been reflecting upon the writing process of the book itself and how the challenges it presented reflect the challenges of a classroom.

There were moments of doubt about the content and the method of systems thinking.

- *Was it too complicated and would practitioners be interested in this different approach?*
- *Have I included enough detail for the resources to be used?*

As you face the challenge of meeting the needs of a cohort with different learning abilities, you might also face the same doubt and concern that what you are implementing is not enough or won't be effective.

Despite these doubts, I have persisted and am confident you will too. Each time I have felt the need to question my approach, I have returned to my purpose which is to encourage practitioners to seek a deeper understanding of their practice and cohorts. Through this understanding, they will find ways which work, but perhaps more importantly, when they hit a stumbling block, they will reflect, step back and reevaluate; not give up.

This book has incorporated years of practice and thousands of hours of deliberation and thought. It builds a system of support which does not require expertise in systems thinking but an open mind, readiness to accept the unknown and an appreciation for multiple perspectives.

As the chapters began to take shape, there were significant changes in the world and the UK, and it is important to be mindful of these events and their potential

DOI: 10.4324/9781003400639-11

impact on both us as individuals but also our environments and the learners. How we manage these changes will determine how confident the learners are in this evolving, uncertain world.

I hope by sharing my journey in writing this book, I give voice to some of the concerns you feel as practitioners and ask you to be kind to yourselves and sit with these feelings, knowing that you don't have to have ALL the answers but urge that you remain curious and open to understanding the situation from multiple perspectives. That you look to iterate an approach, rather than stick to what you know, when you know what you know isn't working. You know?

Knowledge is one thing, but action results in change and that's what most learners who are facing challenges need to happen. Be 10% braver and try something. If it doesn't work, reflect upon it. But what if it does work? Well, that's why we went into education in the first place isn't it?

Take care,
Kelly

Moment of Reflection 10.1: Practice

- What engaged you the most about the book and how does this align with your practice?
- How much did it alter your current practice?
- What was new and useful and why?
- What will change as a result of reading this book?
- Did you complete the reflections, and if no, do you plan to?
- Did you attempt to build the viable systems model?
- Have you shared anything from this book with anyone else?

Index

For Product Safety Concerns and Information please contact our EU representative GPSR@taylorandfrancis.com
Taylor & Francis Verlag GmbH, Kaufingerstraße 24, 80331 München, Germany

www.ingramcontent.com/pod-product-compliance
Lightning Source LLC
LaVergne TN
LVHW010857110826
845149LV00005B/1413

* 9 7 8 1 0 3 2 5 0 9 9 6 9 *